PAINTED WINDOWS

PAINTED WINDOWS

A STUDY IN
RELIGIOUS PERSONALITY

By
HAROLD BEGBIE
(A GENTLEMAN WITH A DUSTER)

It was simply a struggle for fresh air, in which, if the windows could not be opened, there was danger that panes would be broken, though painted with images of saints and martyrs. Light, coloured by these reverend effigies, was none the more respirable for being picturesque. *J. R. Lowell.*

KENNIKAT PRESS
Port Washington, N. Y./London

PAINTED WINDOWS

First published in 1922
Reissued in 1970 by Kennikat Press
Library of Congress Catalog Card No: 77-108696
SBN 8046-0918-7

Manufactured by Taylor Publishing Company   Dallas, Texas

ESSAY AND GENERAL LITERATURE INDEX REPRINT SERIES

CONTENTS

INTRODUCTION

By means of a study in religious personality, I seek in these pages to discover a reason for the present rather ignoble situation of the Church in the affections of men.

My purpose is to examine the mind of modern Christianity, the only religion of the world with which the world can never be done, because it has the lasting quality of growth, and to see whether in the condition of that mind one cannot light upon a cause for the confessed failure of the Church to impress humanity with what its documents call the Will of God—a failure the more perplexing because of the wonderful devotion, sincerity, and almost boundless activity of the modern Church.

As a clue to the object of this quest, I would ask the reader to bear in mind that the present disordered state of the world is by no means a consequence of the late War.

The state of the world is one of confusion, but that confusion is immemorial. Man has for ever been wrestling with an anarchy which has for ever defeated him. The history of the human race is the diary of a Bear Garden. Man, so potent against the mightiest and most august forces of nature, has never been able to subdue those trivial and unworthy forces within his own breast—envy, hatred, malice, and all uncharitableness—which make for world anarchy. He has never been able to love God because he has never been able to love his neighbour. It is in the foremost nations of the world, not in the most backward, in the most Christian nations, not the most pagan, that we find unintelligent conditions of industrialism which lead to social disorder, and a vulgar disposition to self-assertion which makes for war. History and Homicide, it has been said, are indistinguishable terms. " Man is born free, and everywhere he is in chains."

This striking impotence of the human race to arrive at anything in the nature of a coherent world-order, this bewildering incapacity of individual man to live in love and charity with his neighbour, justifies the presumption that divine help, if ever given, that an Incarnation of the Divine Will, if ever vouchsafed, must surely have had for its chief mercy the teaching of a science of life—a way of existence which would bring the feet of unhappy man out of chaos, and finally make it possible for the human race to live intelligently, and so, beautifully.

Now if this indeed were the purpose of the Incarnation, we may be pardoned for thinking that the Church, which has been the cause of so much tyranny and bloodshed in the past, and which even now so willingly lends itself to bitter animosities and warlike controversies, has missed the whole secret of its first and greatest dogma.[1]

[1] I asked a certain Dean the other day whether the old controversy between High Church and Low Church still obtained in his diocese. "Oh, dear, no!" he replied; " High and Low are now united *to fight the Modernists.*"

Therefore in studying the modern mind of Christianity, persuaded that its mission is to teach mankind a lesson of quite sublime importance, we may possibly arrive in our conclusion at a unifying principle which will at least help the Church to turn its moral earnestness, its manifold self-sacrifice, and its great but conflicting energies, in this one direction which is its own supremest end, namely, the interpretation of human life in terms of spiritual reality.

To those who distrust reason and hold fast rather fearfully to the moorings of tradition, I would venture to say, first, that perilous times are most perilous to error, and, secondly, in the words of a noble scholar, " After all, Faith is not belief in spite of evidence, but life in scorn of consequence— a courageous trust in the great purpose of all things and pressing forward to finish the work which is in sight, whatever the price may be."

THE DISTINCTION BETWEEN RIGHT AND
WRONG DISAPPEARS WHEN CONSCIENCE
DIES, AND THAT BETWEEN FACT AND
FICTION WHEN REASON IS NEGLECTED.
THE ONE IS THE DANGER WHICH BESETS
CLEVER POLITICIANS, THE OTHER THE
NEMESIS WHICH WAITS ON POPULAR
PREACHERS.—*Kirsopp Lake.*

PAINTED WINDOWS

Chapter I

BISHOP GORE

He is in truth, in the power, in the hands, of another, of another will . . . attracted, corrected, guided, rewarded, satiated, in a long discipline, that " ascent of the soul into the intelligible world."—Walter Pater.

No man occupies a more commanding position in the Churches of England than Dr. Gore. I am assured in more than one quarter that a vote on this subject would place him head and shoulders above all other religious teachers of our time. In the region of personal influence he appears to be without a rival.

Such is the quality of his spirit, that a person so different from him both in temperament and intellect as the Dean of St. Paul's has confessed that he is " one of the most powerful spiritual forces in our generation."

It is, I think, the grave sincerity of his soul which gives him this pre-eminence. He is not more eloquent than many others, he is not greatly distinguished by scholarship, he is only one in a numerous company of high-minded men who live devout and disinterested lives. But no man conveys, both in his writings and in his personal touch, a more telling sense of ghostly earnestness, a feeling that his whole life is absorbed into a Power which overshadows his presence and even sounds in his voice, a conviction that he has in sober truth forsaken everything for the Kingdom of God.

One who knows him far better than I do said to me the other day, " Charles Gore has not aimed at harmonising his ideas with the Gospel, but of fusing his whole spirit into the Divine Wisdom."

In one, and only one, respect, this salience of Dr. Gore may be likened to the political prominence of Mr. Lloyd George. It is a salience complete, dominating, unapproached, but one which must infallibly diminish with time. For it is, I am compelled to think, the salience of personality. History does not often endorse the more enthusiastic verdicts of journalism, and personal magnetism is a force which unhappily melts into air long before its tradition comes down to posterity.[1]

Mr. Joseph Chamberlain was once speaking to me of the personality of Gladstone. He related with unusual fervour that the effect of this personality was incomparable, a thing quite unique in his experience, something indeed incommunicable to those who had not met the man ; yet, checking himself of a sudden, and as it were shaking himself free of a superstition, he added resolutely, " But I was reading some of his speeches in Hansard only the other day, and upon my word there's nothing in them ! "

[1] The genius of the Prime Minister, which makes so astonishing an impression on the public, plainly lies in saving from irretrievable disaster at the eleventh hour the consequences of his own acts.

One may well doubt the judgment of Mr. Chamberlain; but it remains very obviously true that the personal impression of Gladstone was infinitely greater than his ideas. The tradition of that almost marvellous impression still prevails, but solely among a few, and there it is fading. For the majority of men it is already as if Gladstone had never existed.

We should be wise, then, to examine the mind, and only the mind, of this remarkable prelate, and to concern ourselves hardly at all with the beauty of his life or the bewitchments of his character; for our purpose is to arrive at his value for religion, and to study his personality only in so far as it enables us to understand his life and doctrine.

Dr. Gore lives in a small and decent London house which at all points in its equipment perfectly expresses a pure taste and a wholly unstudied refinement. Nothing there offends the eye or oppresses the mind. It is the dignified habitation of a poor gentleman, breathing a charm not to be found in the house of a rich parvenu. He has avoided without effort the conscious artistry of Chelsea and the indifference to art of the unæsthetic vulgarian. As to the manner of his life, it is reduced to an extreme of simplicity, but his asceticism is not made the excuse for domestic carelessness. A sense of order distinguishes this small interior, which is as quiet as a monk's cell, but restful and gracious, as though continually overlooked by a woman's providence.

Here Dr. Gore reads theology and the newspaper, receives and embraces some of his numerous disciples,

discusses socialism with men like Mr. Tawney,
church government with men like Bishop Temple,
writes his books and sermons, and on a cold day,
seated on a cushion with his feet in the fender and
his hands stretched over a timorous fire, revolves
the many problems which beset his peace of mind.[1]

Somewhere, in speaking of the Church's attitude
towards rich and poor, he has confessed to carrying about with him " a permanently troubled
conscience." The phrase lives in his face. It is
not the face of a man who is at peace with himself.
If he has peace of mind, it is a Peace of Versailles.

One cannot look at that tall lean figure in its
purple cassock, with the stooping head, the somewhat choleric face, the low forehead deeply scored
with anxiety, the prominent light-coloured and
glassy eyes staring with perplexity under bushy
brows, which are as carefully combed as the hair of
his head, the large obstinate nose with its challenging
tilt and wide war-breathing nostrils, the broad
white moustache and sudden pointed beard sloping
inward ; nor can one listen to the deep, tired, and
ghostly voice slowly uttering the laborious ideas
of his troubled mind with the somewhat painful
pronunciation of the elocutionist (he makes *chap-
pell* of Chapel) ; nor mark his languorous movements
and the slow swaying action of the attenuated
body ; one cannot notice all this without feeling
that in spite of his great courage and his iron
tenacity of purpose, he is a little weary of the

---

[1] Concerning modernising tendencies, Father Ronald Knox says,
"I went to a meeting about it in Margaret Street, where crises in the
Church are invested with a peculiar atmosphere of delicious
trepidation."

battle, and sometimes even perhaps conscious of a check for the cause which is far dearer to him than his own life.

One thinks of him as a soul under a cloud. He gives one no feeling of radiance, no sense of a living serenity. What serenity he possesses at the centre of his being does not shine in his face nor sound in his voice. He has the look of one whose head has long been thrust out of a window gloomily expecting an accident to happen at the street corner. FitzGerald once admirably described the face of Carlyle as wearing " a crucified expression." No such bitterness of pain and defeat shows in the face of Dr. Gore. But his look is the look of one who has not conquered and who expects further, perhaps greater disaster.

He has told us that " a man must be strong at the centre before he can be free at the circumference of his being," and in support of this doctrine he quotes the words of Jesus, " It is better to enter into life halt or maimed rather than having two hands or two feet to go into hell." Has he reached strength at the centre, one wonders, by doing violence to any part of his moral being? Is his strength not the strength of the whole man but the strength only of his will, a forced strength to which his reason has not greatly contributed and into which his affections have not entirely entered? Is this, one asks, the reason of that look in his face, the look of bafflement, of perplexity, of a permanently troubled conscience, of a divided self, a self that is both maimed and halt?

How is it, we ask ourselves, that a man who makes

so profound an impression on those who know him, and who commands as no other teacher of his time the affectionate veneration of the Christian world, and who has placed himself whole-heartedly in political alliance with the militant forces of victorious Labour, exercises so little influence in the moral life of the nation ? How is it that he suggests to us no feeling of the elation of triumphant leadership, but rather the spirit of Napoleon on the retreat from Moscow ?

We learn from his teaching that no one can be a Christian without " a tremendous act of choice," that Christ proclaimed His standard with " tremendous severity of claim," that " it is very hard to be a good Christian," and that we must surely, as St. Peter says, " pass the time of our sojourning here in fear." All of which suggests to us that the Bishop has not entered into life whole, even perhaps that sometimes he looks back over his shoulder with a spasm of horror at the hell from which he has escaped only by the sacrifice of his rational integrity.

Let us recall the main events of his history.

He was educated at Harrow and Balliol, and exercised a remarkable spiritual influence at Oxford, where he remained, first as Vice-Principal of Cuddesdon College and then as Librarian of Pusey House, till he was forty years of age.

During these years he edited the book called *Lux Mundi* in which he abandoned the dogma of verbal inspiration and accepted the theory that the human knowledge of Christ was limited. This book distressed a number of timid people, but extended the influence of Dr. Gore to men of science, such as Romanes, as well as to a much larger number of thoughtful undergraduates.

For a year he was Vicar of Radley, and then came to London as a Canon of Westminster, immediately attracting enormous congregations to hear him preach, his sermons being distinguished by a most singular simplicity, a profound piety, and above all by a deep honesty of conviction which few who heard him could withstand. Weller, the Dean's verger at the Abbey, has many stories to tell of the long queues at Westminster which in those days were one of the sights of London. The Abbey has never since recovered its place as a centre of Christian teaching.

Up to this time Dr. Gore's sympathy for the Oxford Movement was merely the background of a life devoted to the mystical element and the moral implications of the Christian religion. He was known as a High Churchman ; he was felt to be a saint ; his modernism was almost forgotten.

It was not long before his tentative movement towards modernism ended in a profession of Catholic principles which allied him with forces definitely and sometimes angrily ranged against the Higher Criticism. He became a Bishop. Almost at once the caressing fingers of the saint became the heavy hand of the dogmatist. He who had frightened Liddon by his tremulous adventure towards the mere fringe of modernism became the declared enemy, the implacable foe, of the least of his clergy who questioned even the most questionable clauses of the creeds. He demanded of them all a categorical assent to the literal truth of the miraculous, in exactly the same sense in which physical facts are true. Every word of the creeds had to be uttered *ex animo*. " It is very hard to be a good Christian." Yes ; but did Dr. Gore make it harder than it need be ? There was something not very unlike a heresy hunt in the diocese over which the editor of *Lux Mundi* ruled with a rod of iron.

I remember once speaking to Dr. Winnington Ingram, Bishop of London, about the Virgin Birth. He told me that he had consulted Charles Gore on this matter, and that he agreed with Charles Gore's ruling that if belief in that miracle were abandoned Christianity would perish. Such is the fate of those who put their faith in dogmas, and plant their feet on the sands of tradition.

Dr. Gore's life as a Bishop, first of Worcester, then of Birmingham, and finally of Oxford, was disappointing to many of his admirers, and perhaps to himself. He did well to retire. But unfortunately this retirement was not consecrated to those exercises which made him so impressive and so powerful an influence in the early years of his ministry. He set himself to be, not an exponent of the Faith, but the defender of a particular aspect of that Faith.

Here, I think, is to be found the answer to our question concerning the loss of Dr. Gore's influence in the national life. From the day of the great sermons in Westminster Abbey that wonderful influence has diminished, and he is now in the unhappy position of a party leader whose followers begin to question his wisdom. Organisation has destroyed him.

Dr. Gore, in my judgment, has achieved strength at the centre of his being only at the terrible cost of cutting off, or at any rate of maiming, his own natural temperament. Marked out by nature for the life of mysticism, he has entered maimed and halt into the life of the controversialist. With the richest of spiritual gifts, which demand quiet and a profound peace for their development, he has thrown himself into the arena of theological disputation, where force of intellect rather than beauty of character is the first requirement of victory. Instead of drawing all men to the sweet reasonableness of the Christian life, he has floundered in the obscurities of a sect and hidden his light under the bushel of a mouldering solecism—" the tradition of Western Catholicism." It is a tragedy. Posterity, I think, will regretfully number him among bigots, lamenting that one who was so clearly

> . . . born for the universe, narrow'd his mind,
> And to party gave up what was meant for mankind.

For, unhappily, this party in the Church to which, as Dean Inge well puts it, Dr. Gore " consents to belong," and for which he has made such manifold sacrifices, and by which he is not always so loyally followed as he deserves to be, is of all parties in the Church that which least harmonises with English temperament, and is least likely to endure the intellectual onslaughts of the immediate future.

It is the Catholic Party, the spendthrift heir of the Tractarians, which, with little of the intellectual

force that gave so signal a power to the Oxford
Movement, endeavours to make up for that sad if
not fatal deficiency by an almost inexhaustible
credulity, a marked ability in superstitious ceremonial, a not very modest assertion of the claims
of sacerdotalism, a mocking contempt for preaching,
and a devotion to the duties of the parish priest
which has never been excelled in the history of the
English Church.

Bishop Gore, very obviously, is a better man
than his party. He is a gentleman in every fibre
of his being, and to a gentleman all extravagance
is distasteful, all disloyalty is impossible. He is,
indeed, a survival from the great and orderly
Oxford Movement trying to keep his feet in the
swaying midst of a revolutionary mob, a Kerensky
attempting to withstand the forces of Bolshevism.

There is little question, I think, that when his
influence is removed, an influence which becomes
with every year something of a superstition, something of an irritation, to the younger generation of
Anglo-Catholics—not many of whom are scholars
and few gentlemen—the party which he has served
so loyally, and with so much distinction, so much
temperance, albeit so disastrously for his own
influence in the world, will perish on the far
boundaries of an extremism altogether foreign to
our English nativity.

For to many of those who profess to follow him
he is already a hesitating and too cautious leader,
and they fret under his coldness towards the millinery
of the altar, and writhe under his refusal to accept
the strange miracle of Transubstantiation—a

miracle which, he has explained, I understand, demands a reversal of itself to account for the change which takes place in digestion. If they were rid of his restraining hand, if they felt they could trust themselves without his intellectual championship, these Bolshevists of sacerdotalism, these enthusiasts for the tyranny of an absolute Authority, these episcopalian asserters of the Apostolical Succession who delight in flouting and defying and insulting their bishops, would soon lose in the follies of excess the last vestiges of English respect for the once glorious and honourable Oxford Movement.

If any man think that I bear too hardly on these very positive protagonists of Latin Christianity, let him read the Anglican chapters in *A Spiritual Æneid*. Father Knox was once a member of this party and something of a disciple of Dr. Gore, who, however, always regretted his " mediæval " theology.

A member of this party, marching indeed at its head and its one voice in these degenerate days to which men of intelligence pay the smallest attention, Bishop Gore has lost the great influence he once exercised, or began to exercise, on the national life, a moral and spiritual influence which might at this time have been well-nigh supreme if the main body of the nation had not unfortunately lost its interest for the man in its contempt for, or rather its indifference to, the party to which he consents to belong.

But for the singular beauty of his spiritual life, one would be tempted to set him up as an example of Coleridge's grave warning, " He, who begins by loving Christianity better than Truth, will proceed by loving his own Sect or Church better than Christianity, and end in loving himself better than all."

I find him in these late days no nearer to Rome, not an inch nearer, than in the days of his early manhood, but absolutely convinced that Christ founded a Church and instituted the two chief sacraments. He will sacrifice nothing in this respect. His whole mind, which is a very different thing from his whole spirit, leans towards authority, order, and coherence. He must have an organised society of believers, believers in the creeds, and he must have an absolute obedience to authority among these believers.

But he is a little shaken and very much alarmed by the march of modernism. " When people run up to you in the street," he said recently, and the phrase suggests panic, " and say, ' Oh ! what are we to do ? ' I have got no short or easy answer at all." A large, important, and learned body of men in the Church, he says, hold views which are " directly subversive of the foundations of the creeds." He calls this state of things evidence of " an extraordinary collapse of discipline." But that is not all. He is alarmed ; he is not content to trust the future of the Church to authority alone. " What are we to do ? " He replies :

" First, we must not be content to appeal to authority. We must teach, fully teach, re-teach the truth on grounds of Scripture, reason, history, everything, so that we may have a party, a body which knows not only that it has got authority, but that it has got the truth and reason on its side."

The claim is obviously courageous, the claim of a brave and noble man, but one wonders, Can it be made good ? It is a long time since evolution saw Athanasius laid in the grave, a long time since the Inquisition pronounced the opinions of Galileo to be heretical and therefore false. " It is very hard to be a good Christian." Did Athanasius make it easier ? Did the Inquisition which condemned Galileo make it easier still ?

Dr. Gore thinks that the supreme mistake of Christianity was placing itself under the protection and patronage of national governments. It should never have become nationalised. Its greatest and most necessitous demand was to stand apart from anything in the nature of racialism.

He mourns over an incoherent humanity ; he seeks for unifying principles. The religion of an Incarnation must have a message for the world, a message for the whole world, for all mankind. Surely, surely. But unifying principles are not popular in the churches. It is the laity which objects to a coherent Gospel.

He sighs for a spiritualised Labour Party. He shrinks from the thought of a revolution, but does not believe that the present industrial system can be Christianised. There must be a fundamental change. Christianity is intensely personal, but its individualism is of the spirit, the individualism of unselfishness. He laughs grimly, in a low and rumbling fashion, on hearing that Communism is losing its influence in the north of England. " I can quite imagine that ; the last thing an Englishman will part with is his property."

Laughter, if it can be called laughter, is rare on his lips, and is reserved in general for opinions which are in antagonism to his own. He laughs in this way at the makeshift compromises of statesmen and theologians and economists, saying that what those men hate more than anything else is a fixed principle. He quotes with a sardonic pleasure the capital saying that a certain statesman's idea of a settled policy based on fixed moral principles is a policy which will last from breakfast-time to luncheon—he repeats the last words " from breakfast-time to luncheon," with a deep relish, an indrawing of the breath, a flash of light in the glassy eyes.

He remains impenitent concerning his first instinct as to England's duty at the violation of Belgium's neutrality. We were justified in fighting ; we could do no other ; it was a stern duty laid upon us by the Providence which overrules the foolishness of man. But he is insistent that we can justify our fiery passion in War only by an equal passion in the higher cause of Peace—no, not an equal passion, a far greater passion.

We lost at Versailles our greatest opportunity for that divine justification. We showed no fervour for peace. There was no passion in us ; nothing but scepticism, incredulity, and the base appetite for revenge. We might have led the world into a new epoch if at that moment we had laid down our sword, taken up our cross, and followed the

Prince of Peace. But we were cold, cold. We had no idealism. We were poor sceptics trusting to economics—the economics of a base materialism.

But though he broods over the sorrows and sufferings of mankind, and views with an unutterable grief the dismemberment of Christendom, he refuses to style himself a pessimist. There is much good in the world; he is continually being astonished by the goodness of individuals; he cannot bring himself to despair of mankind. Ah, if he had only kept himself in that atmosphere! But " it is very hard to be a good Christian."

As for theology, as for modernism, people are not bothered, he says, by a supposed conflict between Religion and Science. What they want is a message. The Catholic Church must formulate a policy, must become intelligent, coherent.

He has small faith in meetings, pronouncing the word with an amused disdain, nor does he attach great importance to preaching, convinced that no Englishman can preach : " Even Roman Catholics can't preach in England." As for those chapels to which people go to hear a popular preacher, he calls them " preaching shops," and speaks with pity of those who occupy their pulpits : " That must be a dreadful life—dreadful, oh, quite dreadful ! " Yet he has a lasting admiration for the sermons of Charles Spurgeon. As to Jeremy Taylor, " I confess that all that turgid rhetoric wearies me."

He does not think the Oxford Movement has spent itself. On the contrary, the majority of the young men who present themselves for ordination are very largely inspired by the spirit of that

Movement. All the same, he perceives a danger in formalism, a resting in symbolism for its own sake. In its genesis, the Oxford Movement threw up great men, very great men, men of considerable intellectual power and a most profound spirituality ; it is not to be expected, perhaps, that such giants should appear again, and in their absence lesser men may possibly mistake the symbol for the thing symbolised, and so fall into the error of formalism. That is a danger to be watched and guarded against. But the Movement will continue, and it will not reach its fulfilment until under its pressure the Church has arrived at unity and formulated a policy intelligent and coherent.

So this great spirit, who might have given to mankind a book worthy to stand beside the *Imitation*, and given to England a new enthusiasm for the moral principles of Christianity, nurses a mechanistic dream and cherishes the hope that his Party is the Aaron's rod of all the Churches. Many would have followed him if he had been content to say only, " Do as I do," but he descended into the dust of controversy, and bade us think as he thinks. Nevertheless, in spite of this fatal mistake he remains the greatest spiritual force among the Churches of England, and his books of devotion will be read long after his works of controversy have fallen into that coldest of all oblivions, the oblivion of inadequate theologies.

CHAPTER II

DEAN INGE

*Some day, when I've quite made up my mind what to fight for, or whom to fight, I shall do well enough, if I.live, but I haven't made up my mind what to fight for—whether, for instance, people ought to live in Swiss cottages and sit on three-legged or one-legged stools ; whether people ought to dress well or ill ; whether ladies ought to tie their hair in beautiful knots ; whether Commerce or Business of any kind be an invention of the Devil or not ; whether Art is a Crime or only an Absurdity ; whether Clergymen ought to be multiplied, or exterminated by arsenic, like rats ; whether in general we are getting on, and if so where we are going to ; whether it's worth while to ascertain any of these things ; whether one's tongue was ever made to talk with or only to taste with.—*JOHN RUSKIN.

WHEN our day is done, and men look back to the shadows we have left behind us, and there is no longer any spell of personal magnetism to delude right, judgment, I think that the figure of Dean Inge may emerge from the dim and too crowded tapestry of our period with something of the force, richness, and abiding strength which gives Dr. Johnson his great place among authentic Englishmen.

His true setting is the Deanery of St. Paul's, that frowning and melancholy house in a backwater of London's jarring tide, where the dust collects, and sunlight has a struggle to make two ends meet, and cold penetrates like a dagger, and fog hangs like a pall, and the blight of ages clings to stone and brick, to window and woodwork, with an adhesive mournfulness which suggests the hatchment of Melpomene. Even the hand of Grinling Gibbons at the porch does not prevent one from recalling Crabbe's memorable lines :

> Dark but not awful, dismal but yet mean,
> With anxious bustle moves the cumbrous scene ;
> Presents no objects tender or profound,
> But spreads its cold unmeaning gloom around.

Here in the midst of overshadowing warehouses —and until he came hither at the age of fifty-one few people in London had ever heard his name, a name which even now is more frequently pronounced as if it rhymed with *cringe*, instead of with *sting*—here the Dean of St. Paul's, looking at one moment like Don Quixote, at another like a figure from the pages of Dostoevsky, and flitting almost noiselessly about rooms which would surely have been filled for the mind of Dickens with ghosts of both sexes and of every order and degree ; here the great Dean faces the problems of the universe, dwells much with his own soul, and fights the Seven Devils of Foolishness in a style which the Church of England has not known since the days of Swift.

In appearance he is very tall, rigid, long-necked, and extremely thin, with fine dark hair and a lean grey clean-shaven face, the heavy-lidded eyes of an almost Asian deadness, the upper lip projecting beyond the lower, a drift of careless hair sticking boyishly forward from the forehead, the nose thin, the mouth mobile but decisive, the whole set and colour of the face stonelike and impassive.

In repose he looks as if he had set himself to stare the Sphinx out of countenance, and not yet had lost heart in the matter. When he smiles, it is as if a mischievous boy looked out of an undertaker's window ; but the smile, so full of wit, mischief, and even gaiety, is gone in an instant, quicker than I have ever seen a smile flash out of sight, and immediately the fine scholarly face sinks back into somnolent austerity which for all its aloofness and immemorial calm suggests, in some fashion for which I cannot account, a frozen whimsicality.

Few public men, with perhaps the exception of Samuel Rogers, ever cared so little about appearance. It is believed that the Dean would be indistinguishable from a tramp but for the constant admonishment and active benevolence of Mrs. Inge. As it is, he is something more than shabby, and only escapes a disreputable appearance by the finest of hairs, resembling, as I have suggested, one of those poor Russian noblemen whom Dostoevsky loved to place in the dismal and sordid atmosphere of a lodging-house, there to shine like golden planets by the force of their ideas.

But when all this is said, and it is worth saying, I hope, if only to make the reader feel that he is here making the acquaintance of an ascetic of the intellect, a man who cares most deeply for accurate thought, and is absorbed body, soul, and spirit

in the contemplation of eternal values, still, for
all the gloom of his surroundings and the deadness
of his appearance, it is profoundly untrue to think
of the Dean as a prophet of pessimism.

When he speaks to one, in the rather muffled
voice of a man troubled by deafness, the impression
he makes is by no means an impression of melancholy
or despair ; on the contrary it is the impression
of strength, power, courage, and unassailable
allegiance to truth. He is careless of appearance
because he has something far better worth the
while of his attention ; he is aloof and remote,
monosyllabic and sometimes even inaccessible,
because he lives almost entirely in the spiritual
world, seeking Truth with a steady perseverance
of mind, Goodness with the full energy of his heart,
and Beauty with the deep mystical passion of his
soul.

Nothing in the man suggests the title of his most
popular book *Outspoken Essays*—a somewhat
boastful phrase that would, I think, have slightly
distressed a critic like Ste.-Beuve—and nothing,
except a certain firm emphasis on the word *truth*,
suggests in his conversation the spirit that shows
in the more controversial of his essays. On the
contrary, he is in manner, bearing, and spirit a
true mystic, a man of silence and meditation,
gentle when he is not angered, modest when he is
not challenged by a fool, humble in his attitude
to God if not to a foolish world, and, albeit with
the awkwardness inevitable in one who lives so
habitually with his own thoughts and his own
silence, anxious to be polite.

" I do not like being unpleasant," he said to me
on one occasion, " but if no one else will, and the
time requires it——"

It is a habit with him to leave a sentence unfinished
which is sufficiently clear soon after the start.

In what way is he unpleasant? and what are
those movements of the time which call in his
judgment for unpleasantness?

Of Bergson he said to me, " I hope he is still
thinking," and when I questioned him he replied
that Bergson's teaching up to this moment " suggests
that anything may happen."

Here you may see one of the main movements
of our day which call, in the Dean's judgment,
for unpleasantness—the unpleasantness of telling
people not to make fools of themselves. Humanity
must not go over in a body to Mr. Micawber.

Anything may happen? No! We are not
characters in a fairy tale, but men of reason, inhabit-
ing a world which reveals to us at every point of
our investigation one certain and unalterable fact—
an unbroken uniformity of natural law. We must
not dream ; we must act, and, before we act, we
must think. Human nature does not change very
greatly. Bergson is apt to encourage easy optimism,
to leave the door open for credulity, superstition,
idle expectation ; and he is disposed to set instinct
above reason, " a very dangerous doctrine, at any
rate for *this* generation."

What is wrong with this generation? It is a
generation that refuses to accept the rule and
discipline of reason, which thinks it can reach
millennium by a short cut, or jump to the moon

in an excess of emotional fervour. It is a generation which becomes a crowd, and "individuals are occasionally guided by reason, crowds never." It is a generation which lives by catchwords, which plays tricks, which attempts to cut knots, which counts heads.

What is wrong with this generation? Public opinion is "a vulgar, impertinent, anonymous tyrant who deliberately makes life unpleasant for anyone who is not content to be the average man." Democracy means "a victory of sentiment over reason"; it is the triumph of the unfit, the ascendancy of the second-rate, the conquest of quality by quantity, the smothering of the hard and true under the feather-bed of the soft and the false.

> Some may prefer the softer type of character, and may hope that it will make civilisation more humane and compassionate. . . . Unfortunately, experience shows that none is so cruel as the disillusioned sentimentalist. He thinks that he can break or ignore nature's laws with impunity; and then, when he finds that nature has no sentiment, he rages like a mad dog, and combines with his theoretical objection to capital punishment a lust to murder all who disagree with him.

Beware of sentiment! Beware of it in politics, beware of it in religion. See things as they are. Accept human nature for what it is. Consult history. Judge by reason and experience. Act with courage.

As he faces politics, so he faces religion.

He desires to rescue Christianity from all the

sentimental vulgarities which have disfigured it
in recent years—alike from the æsthetic extrava-
gances of the ritualist and the organising fussiness
⸻ evangelical ; to rescue it from these obscuring
⸻ to set it clearly before the eyes

⸻ on of thought—a divine
⸻ he only true science of
⸻ he Soul for its journey,
⸻ the presence of God.
⸻ e pursuit of ultimate,
⸻ hing.

⸻ closest attention of the
⸻ at a glance, understood
⸻ a gesture. It is a deep
⸻ of life. It proposes a
⸻ insists that the spiritual
⸻ sets the invisible above
⸻ al above the temporal.
⸻ he lust of accumulation.
⸻ with a choice that is his
⸻ e must decide. He can-
⸻ ammon. Either his life
⸻ ishable values of spiritual
⸻ that perish and the flesh
⸻ et a man choose. Chris-
⸻ natural ideas ; but let
⸻ o the voice of God, and
⸻ al being. Let him not
⸻ vial notions, or to think
⸻ by bawling falsehood at
⸻ im be humble. Let him
⸻ him give all his attention
concerns his soul.

DISC 71-72
MISC-139404
CANCEL NON-STOCK ADD STOCK
12/02/77
B & T ITEM NO. 000356 N
TITLE SEARCH
ITEM—
E ① ②
ACCOUNT NO. U108803
TITLE ID NO.
B & T ORDER NO. 157361
ORDER CLASS 0
ADJ. CODE M
EDITION XXXX
BATCH
XXXXXXXXXXXXXXXXXXXXXXXX

Here again is the aristocratic principle. The average man, until he has disciplined his reason to understand this great matter, must hold his peace ; certainly he must not presume to lay down the law.

When we exclaim against this doctrine, and speak with enthusiasm of the virtues of the poor, Dr. Inge asks us to examine those virtues and to judge of their worth. Among the poor, he quotes, " generosity ranks far before justice, sympathy before truth, love before chastity, a pliant and obliging disposition before a rigidly honest one. In brief, the less admixture of intellect required for the practice of any virtue, the higher it stands in popular estimation."

But we are to love God with all our *mind*, as well as with all our heart.

Does he, then, shut out the humble and the poor from the Kingdom of God ?

Not for a moment. " Ultimately, we are what we love and care for, and no limit has been set to what we may become without ceasing to be ourselves." The door of love stands open, and through that doorway the poor and the ignorant may pass to find the satisfaction of the saint. But they must be careful to love the right things—to love truth, goodness, and beauty. They must not be encouraged to sentimentalise ; they must be bidden to decide. The poor can be debauched as easily as the rich. Many are called, but few chosen.

His main protest is against *the rule* of the ignorant, the democratic principle applied to the *amor intellectualis Dei*. Rich and poor, learned and ignorant, all must accept, with humility, the teaching of the

sentimental vulgarities which have disfigured it
in recent years—alike from the æsthetic extrava-
gances of the ritualist and the organising fussiness
of the evangelical ; to rescue it from these obscuring
unessentials, and to set it clearly before the eyes
of mankind in the pure region of thought—a divine
philosophy which teaches the only true science of
life, a discipline which fits the Soul for its journey,
" by an inner ascent," to the presence of God.
Mysticism, he says, is the pursuit of ultimate,
objective truth, or it is nothing.

Christianity demands the closest attention of the
mind. It cannot be seen at a glance, understood
in a moment, adopted by a gesture. It is a deep
and profound philosophy of life. It proposes a
transvaluation of values. It insists that the spiritual
life is the only true life. It sets the invisible above
the visible, and the eternal above the temporal.
It tears up by the roots the lust of accumulation.
It brings man face to face with a choice that is his
destiny. He must think, he must decide. He cannot serve both God and Mammon. Either his life
must be given for the imperishable values of spiritual
existence or for the meats that perish and the flesh
that will see corruption. Let a man choose. Christianity contradicts all his natural ideas ; but let
him think, let him listen to the voice of God, and
let him decide as a rational being. Let him not
presume to set up his trivial notions, or to think
that he can silence Truth by bawling falsehood at
the top of his voice. Let him be humble. Let him
listen to the teacher. Let him give all his attention
to this great matter, for it concerns his soul.

Here again is the aristocratic principle. The average man, until he has disciplined his reason to understand this great matter, must hold his peace ; certainly he must not presume to lay down the law.

When we exclaim against this doctrine, and speak with enthusiasm of the virtues of the poor, Dr. Inge asks us to examine those virtues and to judge of their worth. Among the poor, he quotes, " generosity ranks far before justice, sympathy before truth, love before chastity, a pliant and obliging disposition before a rigidly honest one. In brief, the less admixture of intellect required for the practice of any virtue, the higher it stands in popular estimation."

But we are to love God with all our *mind*, as well as with all our heart.

Does he, then, shut out the humble and the poor from the Kingdom of God ?

Not for a moment. " Ultimately, we are what we love and care for, and no limit has been set to what we may become without ceasing to be ourselves." The door of love stands open, and through that doorway the poor and the ignorant may pass to find the satisfaction of the saint. But they must be careful to love the right things—to love truth, goodness, and beauty. They must not be encouraged to sentimentalise ; they must be bidden to decide. The poor can be debauched as easily as the rich. Many are called, but few chosen.

His main protest is against *the rule* of the ignorant, the democratic principle applied to the *amor intellec- tualis Dei*. Rich and poor, learned and ignorant, all must accept, with humility, the teaching of the

Master. Plotinus, he points out, was the school-master who brought Augustine to Christ. The greatest of us has to learn. He who would teach should be a learner all his life.

In everything he says and writes I find this desire to exalt Truth above the fervours of emotionalism and the dangerous drill of the formalist. Always he is calling upon men to drop their prejudices and catchwords, to forsake their conceits and sentiments, to face Truth with a quiet pulse and eyes clear of all passion. Christianity is a tremendous thing; let no man, believer or unbeliever, attempt to make light of it.

It is not compassion for the intellectual difficulties of the average man which has made Dr. Inge a conservative modernist, if so I may call him. Senti-ment of no kind whatever has entered into the matter. He is a conservative modernist because his reason has convinced him of the truth of reason-able modernism, because he has " that intellectual honesty which dreads what Plato calls ' the lie in the soul ' even more than the lie on the lips." He is a modernist because he is an intellectual ascetic.

When we compare his position with that of Dr. Gore we see at once the width of the gulf which separates the traditionalist from the philosopher. To Dr. Gore the creeds and the miracles are essential to Christianity. No Virgin Birth, no Sermon on the Mount! No Resurrection of the Body, no Parable of the Prodigal Son! No Descent into Hell, no revelation that the Kingdom of Heaven is within! Need we wonder that Dr. Gore cries out despairingly for more discipline? He summons reason, it is true, but to defend and explain creeds without which there is no Christianity.

To Dr. Inge, on the other hand, it is what Christ said that matters, what He taught that demands our obedience, what He revealed that commands our love. Christianity for him is not a series of extraordinary acts, but a voice from heaven. It is not the Christ of tradition before whom he bows his knee, but the Christ of history, the Christ of faith, the Christ of experience—the living and therefore the evolving Christ. And for him, as for the great majority of searching men, the more the mists of pious *aberglaube* lift, the more real, the more fair, and the more divine becomes the Face of that living Christ, the more close the sense of His companionship.

A friend of mine once asked him, " Are you a Christian or a Neoplatonist ? " He smiled. " It would be difficult to say," he replied. He was thinking, I am sure, of Troeltsch's significant prophecy, and warning, that *the Future of Christian philosophy depends on the renewal of its alliance with Neoplatonism.*

Let no man suppose that the intellectual virtues are outside the range of religion. " Candour, moral courage, intellectual honesty, scrupulous accuracy, chivalrous fairness, endless docility to facts, disinterested collaboration, unconquerable hopefulness and perseverance, manly renunciation of popularity and easy honours, love of bracing labour and strengthening solitude ; these, and many other cognate qualities," says Baron von Hügel, " bear upon them the impress of God and His Christ."

What Dr. Inge, who quotes these words, says of Plotinus declares his own character. He speaks of "the intense honesty of the man, *who never shirks a difficulty or writes an insincere word.*"

But though he is associated in the popular mind chiefly with modernism, Dr. Inge is not by any means only a controversial theologian. Above and beyond everything else, he is a mystic. You may find indications of this truth even in a book like *Outspoken Essays*, but they are more numerous in his two little volumes, *The Church and the Age* and *Speculum Animæ*, and of course more numerous still in his great work on Plotinus.[1] He is far more a mystic than a modernist. Indeed I regard him as the Erasmus of modernism, one so sure of truth that he would trust time to work for his ideas, would avoid fighting altogether, but certainly all fighting that is in the least degree premature. The two thousand years of Christianity, he says somewhere, are no long period when we remind ourselves that God spent millions of years in moulding a bit of old red sandstone.

Meanwhile we have our cocksure little guides, some of whom say to us, "That is primitive, therefore it is good," and others, "This is up-to-date, therefore it is better." Not very wise persons any of them, I fear.

And again, writing of Catholic Modernism in France :

We have given our reasons for rejecting the Modernist attempt at reconstruction. In the first

---

[1] "I have often thought that the unquestionable inferiority of German literature about Platonism points to an inherent defect in the German mind."—*The Philosophy of Plotinus*, p. 13.

place, we do not feel that we are required by sane criticism to surrender nearly all that M. Loisy has surrendered. We believe that the Kingdom of God which Christ preached was something much more than a platonic dream. We believe that He did speak as never man spake, so that those who heard Him were convinced that He was more than man. We believe, in short, that the object of our worship was a historical figure.

I will give a few extracts from *Speculum Animæ*, a most valuable and most beautiful little book, which show the true bent of his mind :

On all questions *about* religion there is the most distressing divergency. But the saints do not contradict each other.

Prayer . . . is " the elevation of the mind and heart to God." It is in prayer, using the word in this extended sense, that we come into immediate contact with the things that cannot be shaken.

Are we to set against such plain testimony the pessimistic agnosticism of a voluptuary like Omar Khayyám ?

There was the Door to which I found no Key. . . .

May it not be that the door has no key because it has no lock ?

The suggestion that in prayer we only hear the echo of our own voices is ridiculous to anyone who has prayed.

The life of Christ was throughout a life of prayer. Not only did He love to spend many hours in lonely communing with His Father, on the mountain-tops, which He was perhaps the first to love, and to choose for this purpose, but His whole life was spent in habitual realisation of God's presence.

Religion is caught rather than taught ; it is the religious teacher, not the religious lesson, that helps the pupil to believe.

What we love, that we see ; and what we see, that we are.

We need above all things to simplify our religion and our inner life generally.

We want to separate the essential from the non-essential, to concentrate our faith upon the pure God-consciousness, the eternal world which to Christ was so much nearer and more real than the world of external objects.

Christ meant us to be happy, happier than any other people.

It is because he is so profoundly convinced of the mystical truth of Christianity, because he has so honestly tried and so richly experienced that truth as a philosophy of life, it is because of this, and not out of a lack of sympathy with the sad and sorrowful, that he opposes himself to the obscurantism of the Anglo-Catholic and the emotional economics of the political reformer.

" The Christian cure," he says, " is the only real cure." The socialist is talking in terms of the old currency, the currency of the world's quantitative standards ; but Christ introduced a new currency, which demonetises the old. Spiritual goods are unlimited in amount ; they are increased by being shared ; and we rob nobody by taking them. He believes with Creighton that " Socialism will only be possible when we are all perfect, and then it will not be needed."

In the meantime, " Christianity increases the

wealth of the world by creating new values." Only
in the currency of Christ can true socialism hope
to pay its way.

We miss the heart and centre of his teaching
if we forget for a moment that it is his conviction
of the sufficiency of Christ's revelation which makes
him so deadly a critic both of the ritualist and the
socialist—two terms which on the former side at
least tend to become synonymous. He would
have no distraction from the mystery of Christ,
no compromise of any kind in the world's loyalty
to its one Physician. Simplify your dogmas ;
simplify your theologies. Christ is your one
essential.

I have spoken to him about psychical research
and the modern interest in spiritualism. " I don't
think much of *that* ! " he replied. Then, in a lower
key, " It was not through animism and necromancy
that the Jews came to believe in immortality."
How did they reach that belief ? " By thinking
things out, and asking the question, Shall not
the Judge of all the earth do right ? "

The answer is characteristic. Dr. Inge has
thought things out ; everything in his faith has
been thought out ; and the basis of all his thinking
is acceptance of absolute values—absolute truth,
absolute goodness, absolute beauty. No breath
from the class-rooms agitated by Einstein can
shake his faith in these absolutes. His Spirit of
the Universe is absolute truth, absolute goodness,
absolute beauty. He is a Neoplatonist, but something more. He ascends into communion with
this Universal Spirit whispering the Name of Christ,

and by the power of Christ in his soul addresses the Absolute as Abba, Father.

No man is freer from bigotry or intolerance, though not many can hate falsity and lies more earnestly. The Church of England, he tells me, should be a national church, a church expressing the highest reach of English temperament, with room for all shades of thought. He quotes Dollinger, "No church is so national, so deeply rooted in popular affection, so bound up with the institutions and manners of the country, or so powerful in its influences on national character." But this was written in 1872. Dr. Inge says now, "The English Church represents, on the religious side, the convictions, tastes, and prejudices of the English gentleman, that truly national ideal of character. . . . A love of order, seemliness, and good taste has led the Anglican Church along a middle path between what a seventeenth century divine called 'the meretricious gaudiness of the Church of Rome and the squalid slutterny of fanatic conventicles.'"

Uniformity, he tells me, is not to be desired. One of our greatest mistakes was letting the Wesleyan Methodists go; they should have been accommodated within the fold. Another fatal mistake was made by the Lambeth Conference, in its insistence on re-ordination. Imagine the Church of England, with two Scotch Archbishops at its head, thinking that the Presbyterians would consent to so humiliating a condition! An interchange of pulpits is desirable; it might increase our intelligence, or at least it should widen our sympathy. He holds a high opinion of the Quakers. " Practical mystics : perhaps they are the best Christians, I mean the best of them."

Modernism, he defines, at its simplest, as personal experience, in contradistinction from authority. The modernist is one whose knowledge of Christ is so personal and direct that it does not depend on miracle or any accident of His earthly life. Rome, he thinks, is a falling power, but she may get back some of her strength in any great industrial calamity—a revolution, for example. Someone once asked him which he would choose, a Black tyranny, or a Red ? He replied, " On the whole, I think a Black." The friend corrected him. " You are wrong. Men would soon emerge from the ruins of a Red tyranny, but Rome never lets go her power till it is torn from her."

His contempt for the idea of reunion with Rome in her present condition is unmeasured. " The notion almost reminds us of the cruel jest of Mezentius, who bound the living bodies of his enemies to corpses." It is the contempt both of a great scholar and a great Englishman for ignorance and a somewhat ludicrous pretension. " The *caput orbis* has become provincial, and her authority is spurned even within her own borders." England could not kneel at this Italian footstool without ceasing to be England.[1]

" A profound reconstruction is demanded," he says, " and for those who have eyes to see has been

[1] "There are, after all, few emotions of which one has less reason to be ashamed than the little lump in the throat which the Englishman feels when he first catches sight of the white cliffs of Dover." *Outspoken Essays*, p. 58.

already for some time in progress. The new type
of Christianity will be more Christian than the
old, because it will be more moral. A number
of unworthy beliefs about God are being tacitly
dropped, and they are so treated because they
are unworthy of Him."

He sees the future of Christianity as a deep moral
and spiritual power in the hearts and minds of men
who have at length learned the value of the new
currency, and have exchanged profession for
experience.

But this Erasmus, far more learned than the
other, and with a courage which far exceeds the
other's, and with an impatience of nature, an
irritability of mind, which the other seldom knew,
is nevertheless patient of change. He does not
lead as decisively as he might. He does not strike
as often as he should at the head of error. Perhaps
he is still thinking. Perhaps he has not yet made
up his mind whether " Art is a Crime or only an
Absurdity," whether Clergymen ought to be
multiplied or exterminated, whether in general
we are getting on, and if so where we are
going to.

I feel myself that his mind is made up, though
he is still thinking and still seeking ; and I attribute
his indecision as a leader, his want of weight in
the affairs of mankind, to one fatal deficiency in
his mysticism. It is, I presume to suggest, a
mysticism which is separated by no gulf from egoism
—egoism of the highest order and the most spiritual
character, but still egoism. In his quest of God
he is not conscious of others. He thinks of mankind

with interest, not with affection. Humanity is a spectacle, not a brotherhood.

When one speaks to him of the confusion and anarchy in the religious world, and suggests how hard it is for the average man to know which way he should follow, he replies : " Yes, I'm afraid it's a bad time for the ordinary man." But then he has laid it down, " There is not the slightest probability that the largest crowd will ever be gathered in front of the narrow gate." Still one could wish that he felt in his heart something of the compassion of his Master for those who have taken the road of destruction.

He attaches great importance to preaching. He does not at all agree with the sneer at " preaching-shops." That is a convenient sneer for the younger generation of ritualists who have nothing to say and who perform ceremonies they don't understand ; not much meaning *there* for the modern man. No ; preaching is a most important office, although no other form of professional work is done anything like so badly. But a preacher who has something to say will always attract intelligent people.

One does not discuss with him the kind of preaching necessary to convert unintelligent people. That would be to take this great philosopher out of his depth.

As for the Oxford Movement, he regards it as a changeling. His grandfather, an archdeacon, was a Tractarian, a friend of Pusey, a scholar acquainted with all the doctors ; but he was not a ritualist ; he did not even adopt the eastward position.

The modern ritualist is hardly to be considered the lineal descendant of these great scholars. " Romanticism, which dotes on ruins, shrinks from real restoration . . . a Latin Church in England which disowns the Pope is an absurdity."

No, the future belongs to clear thinking and rigorous honesty of the intellect.

Dr. Inge began life as the fag of Bishop Ryle at Eton—the one now occupying the Deanery of St. Paul's ; the other the Deanery of Westminster, both scholars and the friendship still remaining. He was a shy and timorous boy. No one anticipated the amazingly brilliant career which followed at Cambridge, and even then few suspected him of original genius until he became Lady Margaret Professor of Divinity in 1907. His attempts to be a schoolmaster were unsuccessful. He was not good at maintaining discipline, and deafness somewhat intensified a nervous irritability which at times puts an enormous strain on his patience. Nor did he make any notable impression as Vicar of All Saints', Ennismore Gardens, a parochial experience which lasted two years. Slowly he made his way as author and lecturer, and it was not until he came to St. Paul's that the world realised the greatness of his mind and the richness of his genius.

As a correction to the popular delusion concerning his temperament and outlook, although, I must confess, there is something about him suggestive of a London Particular, I will quote in conclusion a few of the many witty epigrams which are scattered throughout his pages, showing that he has a sense of humour which is not always discernible in those who would laugh him away as an unprofitable depressionist.

The clerical profession was a necessity when most people could neither read nor write.

Seminaries for the early training of future clergy-men may indeed be established ; but beds of exotics cannot be raised by keeping the gardeners in green-houses while the young plants are in the open air.

It is becoming impossible for those who mix at all with their fellow-men to believe that the grace of God is distributed denominationally.

Like other idealisms, patriotism varies from a noble devotion to a moral lunacy.

Our clergy are positively tumbling over each other in their eagerness to be appointed court-chaplain to King Demos.

A generation which travels sixty miles an hour must be five times as civilised as one which only travels twelve.

It is not certain that there has been much change in our intellectual and moral adornments since pithecanthropus dropped the first half of his name.

I cannot help hoping that the human race, having taken in succession every path except the right one, may pay more attention to the narrow way that leadeth unto life.

It is useless for the sheep to pass resolutions in favour of vegetarianism, while the wolf remains of a different opinion.

After the second century, the apologists for the priesthood are in smooth waters.

Not everyone can warm both hands before the fire of life without scorching himself in the process.

It is quite as easy to hypnotise oneself into imbecility by repeating in solemn tones, " Progress, Democracy, Corporate Unity," as by the blessed word Mesopotamia, or, like the Indians, by repeating the mystic word " Om " five hundred times in succession.

I have lived long enough to hear the *Zeitgeist* invoked to bless very different theories.

. . . as if it were a kind of impiety not to float with the stream, a feat which any dead dog can accomplish. . . .

An appendix is as superfluous at the end of the human cæcum as at the end of a volume of light literature.

The " traditions of the first six centuries " are the traditions of the rattle and the feeding bottle.

In speaking to me last year of the crowded waiting-lists of the Public Schools, he said : " It is no longer enough to put down the name of one's son on the day he is born, one must write well ahead of that : ' I am expecting to have a son next year, or the year after, and shall be obliged if——' The congestion is very great, in spite of the increasing fees and the supertax."

Much of his journalism, by the way, has the education of his children for its excuse and its consecration—children to whom the Dean of St. Paul's reveals in their nursery a side of his character wholly and beautifully different from the popular legend.

There is no greater mind in the Church of England, no greater mind, I am disposed to think, in the English nation. His intellect has the range of an Acton, his forthrightness is the match of

Dr. Johnson's, and his wit, less biting though little less courageous than Voltaire's, has the illuminating quality, if not the divine playfulness, of the wit of Socrates.

But he lacks that profound sympathy with the human race which gives to moral decisiveness the creative energy of the great fighter. A lesser man than Erasmus left a greater mark on the sixteenth century.

The righteous saying of Bacon obstinately presents itself to our mind and seems to tarry for an explanation : " The nobler a soul is, the more objects of compassion it hath."

Chapter III

FATHER KNOX

Our new curate preached, a pretty hopefull young man, yet somewhat raw, newly come from college, full of Latine sentences, which in time will weare off.—John Evelyn.

There is a story that when Father Knox was an undergraduate at Oxford he sat down one day to choose whether he would be an agnostic or a Roman Catholic. " But is there not some doubt in the matter ? " inquired a friend of mine, to whom I repeated the tale. " Did he really sit down and choose, or did he only toss up ? "

The story, of course, is untrue. It has its origin in the delightful wit and brilliant playfulness of the young priest. Everybody loves him, and nobody takes him seriously.

Few men of his intellectual stature have been received with so little trumpet-blowing into the Roman Catholic Church, and none at all, I think, has so imperceptibly retired from the Church of England. For all the interest it excited, the secession of this extremely brilliant person might have been the secession of a sacristan or a pew-opener. He did not so much " go over to Rome " as sidle away from the Church of England.

But this secession is well worth the attention of religious students. It is an act of personality which helps one to understand the theological chaos of the present-time, and a deed of temperament which illumines some of the more obscure movements of religious psychology. Ronnie Knox, as everybody calls him, the eyes lighting up at the first mention of his name, has gone over to the Roman Catholic Church, not by any means with a smile of cynicism on his face, but rather with the sweat of a struggle still clinging to his soul.

He is the son of an Anglican bishop, a good man whose strong evangelical convictions led him, among many other similar activities, to hold missionary services on the sands of Blackpool. His mother died in his infancy, and he was brought up largely with uncles and aunts, but his own home, of which he speaks always with reverence and affection, was a kind and vigorous establishment, a home well calculated to develop his scholarly wit and his love of mischievous fun. Nothing in his surroundings made for gloom or for a Calvinism of the soul. The swiftness of his intellectual development might have made him sceptical of theology in general, but no influence in his home was likely in any way to make him sceptical of his father's theology in particular.

He went to Eton, and the religion in which he had been brought up stood the moral test of the most critical years in boyhood. It never failed him, and he never questioned it. But when that trial was over, and after an illness which shook up his body and mind, he came under the influence of a matron who held with no little force of character the views of the Anglo-Catholic party. These views stole gradually into the mind of the rather effeminate boy, and although they did not make him question the theology of his father for some years, he soon found himself thinking of the religious opinions of his uncles and aunts with a certain measure of superiority.

" I began to feel," he told me, " that I was living in a rather provincial world—the world described by Wells and Arnold Bennett."

This restlessness, this desire to escape into a greater and more beautiful world, pursued him to Oxford, and, for the moment, he found that greater and beautiful world in the life of Balliol. Bishop Ryle, a good judge, has spoken to me of the young man's extraordinary facility at turning English poetry at sight into the most melodious Greek and Latin, and of the remarkable range of his scholarship. He himself has told us of his love of port and bananas, his joy in early morning celebrations in the chapel of Pusey House, his tea-parties, his delight in debates at the Union, of which he became President, and of his many friendships with undergraduates of a witty and flippant turn of mind. Like many effeminate natures, he was glad of opportunities to prove himself a good fellow. In spite of no heel-taps when the port went round, he won the Hertford in 1907, the Ireland and Craven in 1908, and in 1910 took a first in Greats.

He became a Fellow and Lecturer of Trinity College for two years, then its Chaplain for five

years, and, after leading a life of extravagant and
fighting ritualism as an Anglican priest, at the end
of that period, 1917, he retired from the Church of
England and was received into the Church of Rome.

The consolations of Anglo-Catholicism, then,
were insufficient for the spiritual needs of this scion
of the Low Church.

What were those needs ?

Were they, indeed, *spiritual* needs, as he suggests
by the title of his book *A Spiritual Æneid*, or
æsthetic needs, the needs of a temperament ?—a
temperament which used wit and raillery chiefly
as a shield for its shrinking and quivering emotions,
emotions which we must take note of if we are to
understand his secession.

He was at Eton when a fire occurred in one of
the houses, two boys perishing in the flames. He
tells us that this tragedy made an impression on
him, for it fell at a time in his life when " one begins
to fear death." Fear is a word which meets us
even in the sprightly pages of *A Spiritual Æneid*,
a volume perhaps more fitly to be termed " An
Æsthetic Ramp."

He loved to dash out of college through the chill
mists of a November morning to worship with
" the few righteous men " of the University in the
Chapel of Pusey House, which " conveyed a feeling,
to me most gratifying, of catacombs, oubliettes,
Jesuitry, and all the atmosphere of mystery that
had long fascinated me."

He tells us how his nature " craved for human
sympathy and support," and speaks of the God
whom he " worshipped, loved, and feared." He

prayed for a sick friend with " both hands held above the level of my head for a quarter of an hour or more." He was a Universalist " recoiling from the idea of hell." He believed in omens, though he did not always take them, and was thoroughly superstitious. " The name of Rome has always, for me, stood out from any printed page merely because its initial is that of my own name." " At the time of my ordination I took a private vow, which I always kept, never to preach without making some reference to Our Lady, by way of satisfaction for the neglect of other preachers." He was a youth when he took the vow of celibacy. He had the desire, he tells us, to make himself thoroughly uncomfortable—as Byron would say, " to merit Heaven by making earth a Hell." His superstitions were often ludicrous even to himself. On one occasion in boyhood, he was trying to get a fire to burn : " Let this be an omen," he said. " If I can get this fire to burn, the Oxford Movement was justified."

A visit to Belgium hastened the inevitable decision of such a temperament :

> . . . the extraordinary devotion of the people wherever we went, particularly at Bruges, struck home with a sense of immeasurable contrast to the churches of one's own country. . . .

He did not apparently feel the moral contrast between Belgian and English character.

> . . . The tourist, I know, thinks of it as *Bruges la Morte*, but then the tourist does not get up for early Masses ; he would find life then . . . he can at least go on Friday morning to the chapel of the Saint

Sang and witness the continuous stream of people
that flows by, hour after hour, to salute the relic
and to make their devotions in its presence ; he
would find it hard to keep himself from saying, like
Browning at High Mass, " This is too good not to be
true."

Might he not perhaps say with another great
man, " What must God be if He is pleased by
things which simply displease His educated
creatures ? " In a country where the churches
were once far more crowded than in Belgium, I
was told by a discerning man, Prince Alexis
Obolensky, a former Procurator of the Holy Synod,
that all such devotion is simply superstition. He
said he would gladly give me all Russia's spirituality
if I could give him a tenth of England's moral
earnestness. And he told me this story :

A man set out one winter's night to murder an old
woman in her cottage. As he tramped through the
snow with the hatchet under his blouse, it suddenly
occurred to him that it was a Saint's Day. In-
stantly he dropped on his knees in the snow, crossed
himself violently with trembling hands, and in a
guilty voice implored God to forgive him for his evil
intention. Then he rose up, refreshed and forgiven,
postponing the murder till the next night.

Undoubtedly, I fear, the devotion of priest-
ridden countries, which evokes so spectacular an
effect on the stranger of unbalanced judgment, is
largely a matter of superstition ; how many prayers
are inspired by a lottery, how many candles lighted
by fear of a ghost ?

But Father Knox, whose æsthetic nature had
early responded with a vital impulse to Gothic

architecture and the pomp and mystery of priestly ceremonial, felt in Bruges that the spirit of the Chapel of the Sacred Blood must be introduced into the Church of England " to save our country from lapsing into heathenism." What, I wonder, is his definition of that term, heathenism ?

Bruges had a decisive effect, not only on his æsthetic impulses, but on his moral sense. His conduct as an Anglican priest was frankly that of a Roman propagandist. I do not know that any words more damning to the Romish spirit have ever been written than those in which this most charming and brilliant young man tells the story of his treachery to the Anglican Church. Of celebrating the Communion service he says :

> . . . my own principle was, whenever I spoke aloud, to use the language of the Prayer Book, when I spoke *secreto*, to use the words ordered by the Latin missal.

He said of his propaganda work at this time :

> The Roman Catholics . . . have to serenade the British public from the drive ; we Anglican Catholics have the *entrée* to the drawing-room.

His enthusiasm for the Roman service was such that in one place

> I had to travel for three quarters of an hour to find a church where my manner of celebrating, then perhaps more reminiscent of the missal than of the Prayer Book, was tolerated even in a Mass of Devotion.
>
> About this time I celebrated at a community chapel.

One of the brethren was heard to declare afterwards that if he had known what I was going to do he would have got up and stopped me.

At the conclusion of one of his celebrations abroad, an Englishman in the congregation exclaimed, " Thank God that's over." After his first sermon in Trinity Chapel, an undergraduate (" afterwards not only my friend but my penitent ") was heard to declare excitedly : " Such fun ! The new Fellow's been preaching heresy—all about Transubstantiation."

Such fun ! This note runs through the whole of *A Spiritual Æneid*. A thoroughly undergraduate spirit inspires every page save the last. Religion is treated as a lark. It is full of opportunities for plotting and ragging and pulling the episcopal leg. One is never conscious, not for a single moment, that the author is writing about Jesus of Nazareth, Gethsemane, and Calvary. About a Church, yes ; about ceremonial, about mysterious rites, about prayers to the Virgin Mary, about authority, and about bishops ; yes, indeed ; but about Christ's transvaluation of values, about His secret, about His religion of the pure heart and the childlike spirit, not one single glimpse.

Now let us examine his intellectual position.

In the preface to *Some Loose Stones*,[1] written before he went over to Rome, he explains his position to the modernist :

> . . . there are limits defined by authority, within which theorising is unnecessary and speculation forbidden.

[1] An answer to the volume called *Foundations*.

But I should like here to enter a protest against the assumption . . . that the obscurantist, having fenced himself in behind his wall of prejudices, enjoys an uninterrupted and ignoble peace.

The soldier who has betaken himself to a fortress is thereby in a more secure position than the soldier who elects to fight in the open plain. He has ramparts to defend him. But he has, on the other hand, ramparts to defend. . . . For him there is no retreat.

The whole position stands or falls by the weakest parts in the defences ; give up one article of the Nicene Creed, and the whole situation is lost ; you go under, and the flag you loved is forfeit.

And yet :

I can feel every argument against the authenticity of the Gospels, because I know that if I approached them myself without faith I should as likely as not brush them aside impatiently as one of a whole set of fables.

They would be fables to him unless he approached them with faith. And what is faith ? He tells us in the same preface : " Faith is to me, not an intellectual process, but a divine gift, a special privilege."

It is fair to say that he would now modify this definition, for he has told me that it is a heresy to exclude from faith the operations of the intellect. But the words were written when he was fighting the battle of the soul, written almost on the same page as that which bears these words :

You have not done with doubt, because you have thrown yourself into the fortress ; you are left to keep doubt continually at bay, with the cheerful assurance that if you fail, the whole of your religious life has been a ghastly mistake . . .

for this reason, they have, I think, a notable
significance.

Is it not probable that Father Knox has thrown
himself into a fortress, not out of any burning
desire to defend it, but solely to escape from the
enemy of his own soul? Is it not probable that
he was driven from the field by Fear rather than
summoned to the battlements by Love?

I find this inference justified in numerous ways,
and I do not think on the whole that Father Knox
himself would deny it.   But chiefly I find it justified
by the form and substance of his utterances since
he became a Roman Catholic—fighting and most
challenging utterances which for me at any rate
are belied, and tragically belied, by a look in his
eyes which is unmistakably, I am forced to think,
the look of one who is still wrestling with doubt,
one, I would venture to hazard, who may even
occasionally be haunted by the dreadful fear that
his fortress is his prison.

On the day that Newman entered that fortress
the triumphant cry of St. Augustine rang in his
ears, *Securus judicat orbis terrarum* ; but later came
the moan *Quis mihi tribuat,* and later still the stolen
journey to Littlemore and that paroxysm of tears
as he leaned over the lych-gate looking at the
church.

Not long ago I went one Sunday evening to
Westminster Cathedral. It was winter, and the
streets of tall and sullen houses in that gloomy
neighbourhood were darkening with fog. This
fog crept slowly into the cathedral. The surpliced
boy who presented an alms-dish just within the

doors was stamping his feet and snuffling with cold. The leaves of tracts and pamphlets on the table blew up and chattered in the wind every time the door was thrust open.

The huge building was only half filled, perhaps hardly that. Through the fog it was not easy to see the glittering altar, and when three priests appeared before it their vestments so melted into the cloth that they were visible only when they bowed to the monstrance. The altar bell rang snappishly through this cold fog like the dinner bell of a boarding house, and in that yellow mist, which deepened with every minute, the white flames of the candles lost nearly all their starlike brightness. There seemed to be depression and resentment in the deep voices of the choir rumbling and rolling behind the screen ; there seemed to be haste, a desire to get it over, in the nasal voice of the priest praying almost squeakily at the altar.

People were continually entering the cathedral, many of them having the appearance of foreigners, many of them young men who looked like waiters : one was struck by their reverence, and also by their look of intellectual apathy.

Father Knox appeared in the pulpit, which is stationed far down the nave, having come from his work of teaching at Ware to preach to the faithful at Westminster. He looked very young, and rather apprehensive, a slight boyish figure, swaying uneasily, the large luminous eyes, of an extraordinary intensity, almost glazed with light, the full lips, so obviously meant for laughter, parted with a nervous uncertainty, a wave of thick brown

hair falling across the narrow forehead with a look
of tiredness, the long slender hands never still for
a moment.

I will endeavour to summarise his remarkable
sermon, which was delivered through the fog in a
soft and throaty voice, the body of the preacher
swaying monotonously backward and forward,
the congregation sitting back in its little chairs and
coughing inconveniently from beginning to end. It
was the strangest sermon I have listened to for many
years, and all the stranger for its unimpassioned
delivery.

He spoke of the Fall of Man as a certainty.[1] He
spoke continually of an offended God. Between
this offended God and His creature Man sin had
dug an impassable chasm. But Christ had thrown
a bridge, from heaven's side of that chasm, over
the dreadful gulf. This is why Christ described
Himself as the Way. He is the Way over that
chasm, and there is no other.

But Christ also described Himself as a door.
What is the definition of a door? It is not enough
to say that a door is a thing for letting people in
and letting people out. It is a thing for letting
some people in, and for shutting other people out.

To whom did Christ entrust the key of this
door? To St. Peter—to the disciple who had
denied Him thrice. What a marvellous choice!
Would you have thought of doing that? Should

---

[1] " It is a very singular and important fact that, from the appearance in Genesis of the account of the creation and sin and punishment
of the first pair, not the faintest explicit allusion to it is subsequently
found anywhere in literature until about the time of Christ. . . . Jesus
Himself never once alludes to Adam, or to any part of the story of
Eden."—ALGER.

I have thought of doing that? Would any theologian have invented such an idea? But that is what Christ did.

And ever since, St. Peter and his successors have held the keys of Heaven and Hell, with power to loose and bind. What? you exclaim, were the Keys of Heaven and Hell entrusted to even those Popes who lived sinful lives and brought disgrace on the name of religion? Yes. To them and to no others in their day. Whatever their lives may have been at other moments, when they were loosing and binding they were acting for St. Peter, who stood behind them, and behind St. Peter stood Jesus Christ.

Such in brief was the sermon delivered that Sunday evening to the faithful in Westminster Cathedral by one of the wittiest men now living and one of the cleverest young men who ever came down from Oxford with the assurance of a great career before them.

How is it that he has come to such a pass?

I feel that he is in part whistling to keep up his courage, but in chief forcing himself to utter an extreme of traditional belief in order to destroy the last vestige in his mind of a free intellectual existence. Auto-suggestion has a power of which we only begin to know the first movements.

The man who has said that he would not choose as the battleground of the Christian religion either " the credibility of Judges or the edibility of Jonah," the man who is blest with an unusual sense of humour and intellectual subtlety of a rare order, is here found preaching a theology which is fast being rejected by the students of Barcelona and is being questioned even by the peasants of Ireland. What does it mean ?   Is it possible to understand such a perversion of mind ?

His intellectual position, as he states it, is a simple one—for the present.

He asks us, Is Truth something which we are ordered to keep, or something which we are ordered to find ?

Is our business holding the fort ?   Or is it looking for the Pole ?

The traditionalist can say, " Here is the Truth, written down for you and me in black and white ; I mean to keep it, and defend it from attack ; will you rally round it ?   Will you help me ? "

He shows you the modernist wandering in the wilderness of speculative theology looking for the Truth which the traditionalist, safe, warm, and secure of eternal life, keeps whole and undefiled in his fortress.

It is like a fairy tale.

How simple it sounds !   But when Father Knox looks in the glass does he not see its staring fallacy ?

Did he keep the Truth of his boyhood—the Truth of his father's church ?   Did he not go outside the fortress of Evangelicalism and seek for Truth in the fortress of Anglo-Catholicism ?   And here again, did he not break faith, and once more seek Truth outside its walls ?   If Truth is not something to be found, how is it that he is not still in the house of his fathers ?

Does he fail to see that this argument not merely

explains but vindicates the rejection of Christ by the Jews ? They had their tradition, a tradition of immemorial sanctity, perhaps the noblest tradition of any people in the world.

Does he not also see that it destroys the *raison d'être* of the Christian missionary, and would reduce the whole world to a state of what Nietzsche called Chinaism and profound mediocrity ?

Every religion in history, from the worship of Osiris, Serapis, and Mithras to the loathsome rites practised in the darkness of African forests, has been handed down as unquestionable truth commanding the loyalty of its disciples. What logic, what magic of holiness, could destroy a false religion if tradition is sacrosanct and all innovation of the devil ?

The intellectual duty of a Christian, Father Knox lays it down, is " to resist the natural tendencies of his reason, and believe what he is told, just as he is expected to do what he is told, not what comes natural to him."

Such a proposition provokes a smile, but in the case of this man it provokes a feeling of grief. I cannot bring myself to believe that he has yet found rest for his soul, or that he can so easily strangle the free existence of his mind. His present position fills me with pity, his future with apprehension.

He is one of the modestest of men, almost shrinking in his diffidence and nervous self-distrust, an undergraduate who is mildly excited about an ingenious line of reasoning, a wit who loves to play tricks with the subtlety of a curiously agile brain, a casuist

who sees quickly the chinks in the armour of an
adversary. But with all his boyishness, and charm,
and humility, and engaging cleverness, there is a
light in his eyes too feverish for peace of mind. I
cannot prevent myself from thinking that his
secession, which was something of a comedy to his
friends, may prove something of a tragedy to him.

He seems to me one of the most pathetic examples
I ever encountered of the ruin wrought by Fear.
I think that the one motive of his life has been a
constant terror of finding himself in the wrong.
The door, which for Dr. Inge has no key, because
it has no lock, is to Ronald Knox a door of terror
which opens only to a single key—and a door which
as surely shuts out from eternal life the soul that is
wrong as the soul that is wicked. He must have
certainty. He dare not contemplate the prospect
of awaking one day to find his religious life " a
ghastly mistake."

At the cross roads there was for him no Good
Shepherd, only the dark shadow of an offended
God. He ran for safety, for certainty. Has he
found them ?

It may be that the last of his doubts will leave
him, that the iron discipline of the Roman Church
and the auto-suggestion of his own earnest passion
for inward peace, may deliver him from all fear, all
uneasiness, and that one day, forsaking the challenging sermon and the too violent assertion of the
Catholic faith, he may find himself sitting down in
great peace of mind and with a golden mellowness
of spirit to write an *Apologia pro Vita Sua* more
genial and less shallow than *A Spiritual Æneid*.

Such a book from his pen would lack, I think, the fine sweetness of Newman's great work, but it might excel all other books of religious autobiography in charming wit and endearing good humour. The Church of Rome has caught in him neither a Newman nor a Manning. It has caught either a Sydney Smith or a Tartar.

He has too much humour to be a bigot, and too much humanity to be satisfied with a cell. For the moment he seems to embrace Original Sin, to fling his arms round the idea of an offended God, and to shout at the top of his voice that there is no violence to his reason and to his common sense which he cannot contemplate and most gladly accomplish, in the name of Tradition ; but the pulses cool, the white heat of enthusiasm evaporates, fears take wing as we grow older, and whispers from the outer world of advancing and conquering men find their way into the oldest blockhouse ever built against the movements of thought.

" Science," says Dr. Inge, " has been the slowly advancing Nemesis which has overtaken a barbarised and paganised Christianity. She has come with a winnowing fan in her hand, and she will not stop till she has thoroughly purged her floor."

I am sure Ronald Knox was never meant to shut his eyes and stop his ears against this movement of truth, and I am almost sure that he will presently find it impossible not to look, and not to listen.

And then . . . what then ?

CHAPTER IV

DR. L. P. JACKS

*As an excellent amateur huntsman once said to me,
" If you must cast, lead the hounds into the belief that they
are doing it themselves."*—JOHN ANDREW DOYLE.

ONE of the great ladies of Oxford was telling me
the other day that she remembers a time when
friends of hers refused, even with averted eyes
and a bottle of smelling salts at the nose, to go down
the road where Mansfield College had presumed
to raise its red walls of Nonconformity.

To-day Manchester College, the seat of Unitarianism, stands on this same dissenting road, and
thither the ladies of Oxford go up in great numbers
to listen to the beautiful music which distinguishes
the chapel service, the chapel itself already beautiful
enough with windows by Burne-Jones.

On the altar-cloth of this chapel are embroidered
the words, GOD IS LOVE. No tables of stone
flank that gentle altar, and no panelled creeds on
the walls challenge the visitor to define his definitions. The atmosphere of the place is worship.
The greatest of all Christ's affirmations is reckoned
enough. God is love. No need, then, to add—

Therefore with Angels, and Archangels, and all
the Company of Heaven . . .

The Principal of Manchester College is Dr. L. P.
Jacks, the Editor of *The Hibbert Journal*, the
biographer of Stopford Brooke and Charles Hargrove,
author of *Mad Shepherds*, *Legends of Smokeover*, and
other books which have won the affection of many
readers and the praise of no few scholars. He is a
man of letters, a man of nature, and a mystic.

His face bears a strange resemblance to the
unforgettable face of that great Unitarian, James
Martineau, whom Morley calls " the most brilliant
English apologist of our day " ; it lacks the
marvellous sweetness of Martineau's expression,
but has a greater strength ; it does not bear witness
to so sure a triumph of serenity, but shows the
marks of a fiercer battle, and the scars of deeper
wounds. It is the masculine of the other's feminine.

Like Martineau's the head with its crown of white
hair is nobly sculptured, and like Martineau's the
ivory coloured face is ploughed up and furrowed
by mental strife; but whereas Martineau's is
eminently the indoors face of a student, this is the
face of a man who has lived out of doors, a moun-
taineer and a seafarer. Under the dense bone of
the forehead which overhangs them like the eave
of a roof, the pale blue eyes look out at you with a
deep inner radiance of the spirit, but from the midst
of a face which has been stricken and has winced.

Something of the resolution, the deliberateness,
the stern power, and the enduring strength of his
spirit shows itself, I think, in the short thickset
body, with its heavy shoulders, its deep chest, its

broad firm upright neck, and its slow movements, the movements as it were of a peasant. Always there is about him the feeling of the fields, the sense of nature's presence in his life, the atmosphere of distances. Nothing in his appearance suggests either the smear or the burnish of a town existence.

It is not without significance that he has gone farther afield from Oxford City than any other of its academic citizens, building for himself a home on a hill two miles and more from Magdalen Bridge, with a garden about it kept largely wild, and seats placed where the eye can travel farthest.

This man, who is so unpushing and self-effacing, makes a contribution to the Christian religion which deserves, I think, the thoughtful attention of his contemporaries. It can be set forth in a few words, for his faith is fastened in the conviction that the universe is far simpler than science—for the moment—would allow us to think.

Let me explain at the outset that Unitarianism admits of a certain diversity of faith. There are Unitarians who think and speak only of God. There are others who lay their insistence on the humanity of Jesus, exalting Him solely as the chiefest of teachers. There are others who choose to dwell on the uniqueness of Jesus, who feel in Him some precious but quite inexpressible, certainly quite indefinable, spell of divinity, and who love to lose themselves in mystical meditations concerning His continual presence in the human spirit. Dr. Jacks, I think, is to be numbered among these last. But, like all other Unitarians, he makes no credal demands on mankind, save only the one affirmation of their common faith, with its inevitable ergo : God is Love, and therefore to be worshipped.

Robert Hall said to a Unitarian minister who always baptised " in the Name of the Father and of the Son and of the Holy Ghost," attaching a very sacred meaning to the words, " Why, sir, as I understand you, you must consider that you baptise in the name of an abstraction, a man, and a metaphor." More simple was the interpretation of a Japanese who, after listening with a corrugated brow to the painful exposition of a recent Duke of Argyll concerning the Trinity in Unity, and the Unity in Trinity, suddenly exclaimed with radiant face, " Ah, yes, I see, a Committee."

Dr. Jacks leaves these perplexities alone. For him, God is the Universal Spirit, the Absolute Reality immanent in all phenomena, the Love which reason finds in Goodness and intuition discovers in Beauty, the Father of men, the End and the very Spirit of Evolution. And Jesus, so far as human thought can reach into the infinite, is the Messenger of God, the Revealer both of God's Personality and man's immortality, the great Teacher of liberty. What else He may be we do not know, but may discover in other phases of our ascent. Enough for the moment of duration which we call human life to know that He unlocks the door of our prison-house, reveals to us the character of our Father which is in Heaven, and the nature of the universe in which we move and have our being.

If this should appear vague to the dogmatist who finds it impossible either to love God or to do the will of Christ without going into the arithmetic of Athanasius, and reciting an unintelligible creed, and celebrating in Christian forms the rites of those mystery religions which competed with each other for the superstition of the Græco-Roman world in the third century, he will find no vagueness at all in Dr. Jacks's interpretation of the teaching of Jesus. He may perhaps find in that interpretation a simplicity, a clarity, and a directness which are not wholly convenient to his idea of a God Who repents, is angry, and can be mollified.

Whether Jesus was born of a Virgin or not, whether He raised dead bodies to life or not, whether He Himself rose from the grave with His physical body or not, certain is it, and beyond all dispute of every conceivable kind, that He taught men a way of life, that He brought them a message, that He Himself regarded His message as good news.

How carelessly men may think in this matter is shown to us rather strikingly in a page of *Some Loose Stones*, a book to which reference has already been made. After writing about dogma, and endeavouring to show that the traditionalist is on firmer ground than the modernist, because he can say, " Here is the Truth," while the modernist can only say, " We will tell you what the truth is when we have found it," suddenly, with scarcely a draw of his breath, Father Knox exclaims :

> The real trouble is that they (the modernists) have got hold of the wrong end of the stick, that they have radically misconceived the whole nature of the Christian message, which is, to be one for all minds, for all places, for all times.

Note that word *message*. What confusion of thought!

The message of Christ is one thing; paganised dogma concerning Christ is another. The message of Christ does indeed remain for all minds, for all places, for all times, inexhaustible in its meaning, unalterable in its nature; the dogmas of theology, on the other hand, demand Councils of the Church for their definition, and an infallible Pope for their interpretation. They change, have changed even in the unchangeable Catholic Church, and will change with every advance of the positive sciences and with every ascent of philosophy towards reality; but the message stands, plain to the understanding of a child, yet still rejected by the world. Christianity, as Dr. Jacks says, has been more studied than practised.

How far quarrelling theologians and uncharitable Churches are responsible for that rejection, let the conscience of the traditionalist (if he happen to know history) decide.

As for the message, here is a reading of it by a Unitarian—a reading, I venture to say, for all minds, for all places, for all times—a reading which stands clear of controversial theology, and which, in spite of its profundity, is a message for the simple as well as for the learned.

Christianity is man's passport from illusion into reality. It reveals to him that he is not in the world to set the world right, but to see it right. He is not a criminal and earth is not a Borstal Institution. Nature is the handiwork of a Father. Look deeply into that handiwork and it reveals a threefold tendency—the tendency towards goodness, the tendency towards beauty, the tendency towards truth. Ally yourself with these tendencies, make yourself a growing and developing intelligence, and you inhabit spiritual reality.

Study the manner of Jesus, His attitude to the simplest and most domestic matters, the love He manifested, and the objects for which He manifested that love. These things have " a deeper significance than our pensive theologies have dared to find in them. . . . They belong not to the fringe of Christianity but to its essence." Christ loved the world.

His religion, which has come to stand for repression founded on an almost angry distrust of human nature, is in fact " the most encouraging, the most joyous, the least repressive, and the least forbidding of all the religions of the world." It does not fear the world, it masters it. It does not seek to escape from life, it develops a truer and more abundant life. It places itself at the head of evolution.

There are points on its path where it enters the shadows and even descends into hell, for it is a religion of redemption, the religion of the shepherd seeking the lost sheep, but " the end of it all is a resurrection and not a burial, a festival and not a funeral, an ascent into the heights and not a lingering in the depths."

Nowhere else is the genius of the Christian Religion so poignantly revealed than in the Parable of the Prodigal Son, which begins in the minor key and gradually rises to the major, until it culminates in a great merry-making, to the surprise of the Elder Son, who thinks the majesty of the moral law will be compromised by the music and dancing, and has to be reminded that these joyous sounds are the key-notes of the spiritual world.

Dr. Jacks well says that we should be nearer the truth if, instead of thinking how we can adapt this religion to the minds of the young, we regarded it as " originally a religion of the young which has lost some of its savour by being adapted to the minds of the old."

Then he reminds us that it was " in the form of a person that the radiance of Christianity made its first appearance and its first impression on the world." A Light came into the world.

The Jesus of history drew men to Him by an inward beauty. His serenity gave the sick and the suffering an almost riotous confidence that He could heal them. His radiance attracted children to His side. He was fond of choosing a child for the sub-limest of teachings. He made it clear that entrance into the Kingdom of Heaven is easiest to those who are least deluded or enchained by appear-ances, and hardest to those whose hearts lie in their possessions. The Kingdom of Heaven signifies freedom.

He was the great teacher of the poverty of riches, and the wealth of nothingness. He knew as no other had ever known, and saw as no other had ever seen, the symbolism of nature. Always His vision pierced behind the appearance to the thing in itself. He loved " the reality that abides beyond the shadows." He directed our spiritual vision to this reality, telling us that the soul makes a natural response " to a world built on the same heavenly pattern with itself and aglow with the same immortal fire." He taught that joy is a thing of the spirit. He made it plain that loss, disillusion, and defeat are the penalty of affections set on the outside of things. The materialist is in prison.

He did not condemn the earth ; He taught that its true loveliness is to be discerned only by the spiritual eye. For Him the earth was a symbol, and the whole realm of nature a parable.

> I cannot but think that we are never further from the genius of the Christian religion than when we treat this luminous atmosphere as though it were a foreign envelope, of little account so long as the substance it enshrines is retained intact. Without it, the substance, no matter how simple or how complex, becomes a dry formula, dead as the moon.

> Losing the radiance we lose at the same time the central light from which the radiance springs, and our religion, instead of transforming the corruptible world into its incorruptible equivalents, reverts to the type it was intended to supersede and becomes a mere safeguard to the moral law.

Nothing can allay our present discords and the long confusions of the world, short of " those radiant conceptions of God, of man, of the universe, which are the life and essence of Christianity."

" Liberty," says Edouard Le Roy, " is rare ; many live and die and have never known it." And Bergson says, " We are free when our acts proceed from our entire personality, when they express it, when they exhibit that indefinable resemblance to it which we find occasionally between the artist and his work."

This, I think, is what Dr. Jacks means when he speaks of Christianity bestowing liberty—a new mastery over fate and circumstance. It calls forth not only the affection of a man, and not only the intelligence of a man, but the whole of his intuitions as well. The entire personality, the entire field of consciousness, the entire mystery of the ego, is bidden to throw itself upon the universe with confidence, with gratitude, with love unspeakable, recognising there the act of a Fatherhood of which, in its highest moments, the soul is conscious in itself.

Thus is man made free of illusion. No longer can the outside of things deceive him, or the defeats of the higher by the lower deject, much less overwhelm him. He sees the reality behind the appearance. He dwells with powers which are invisible and eternal—with justice, with virtue, with beauty, with truth, with love, with excellence. More to him than any house built with hands, more, much more even than the habitation of his own soul, is the invisible life of that soul, its delight in beauty, its immediate response to truth and goodness, its longing for the flight of the One to the One, its almost athletic sense of spiritual fitness.

Dr. Jacks will have no element of fear in this religion. He finds no room in the universe for an offended God. Belief in God can mean nothing else but love of God. All our troubles have come upon us from the failure of the Church to live in the radiant atmosphere of this belief, to make belief a life, a life that needs no dogmas and expresses itself by love.

But this was not to be. The Church cultivated fear of God, and could not bring itself to trust human nature.

> Belief passed into dogma ; the mind of man was put in fetters as well as his body ; the Church built one prison and the State another. . . . All this was closely connected with the idea of the *potentate* God which Church and State, in consequence of their political alliance, had restored, against the martyr protest of Jesus Christ.

But how should man be treated? Here it is that Dr. Jacks makes a most valuable suggestion :

> Treat man, after the mind of Christ, as a being whose first need is for Light, and whose second need is for government, and you will find that as his need for light is progressively satisfied, his need for government will progressively diminish.
>
> Is it not a significant fact that while the churches are complaining of emptiness, the schools, the colleges, the universities, are packed to overflowing?

Dr. Jacks has asked quite recently a Frenchman, a Swede, a Dutchman, an American, a Chinaman, and a Japanese, " What is the leading interest in your country ? What do your people really believe in ? " The answer in each case was, " Education." When he varied his question, and asked, " What have you learnt from the war ? " the answer came, " We have learnt our need of education."

> Some would prefer them to have said : " We have learnt our need of Christianity." But is it not the same thing ? In grasping the vast potentialities of the human spirit, and that is what this hunger for education means, have they not grasped an essential

characteristic of the Christian religion and placed themselves at its very growing point?

Education is Light, and Light is from God.

Dr. Jacks believes that a movement has begun which, " if it develops according to promise, will grow into the most impassioned enterprise so far undertaken by man."

The struggle for *light*, with its wide fellowships and high enthusiasms, will displace the struggle for *power*, with its mean passions, its monstrous illusions, and its contemptible ideals.

The struggle for power will end, not, as some predict, in universal revolution, which would merely set it going again in another form, but by being submerged, lost sight of, snowed under, by the greater interests that centre round the struggle for light.

I say these things will happen. But they will not happen unless men are sufficiently resolved that they shall.

Let the reader remember that those who now flock to the schoolmaster are less likely than men of the previous generation to fall into the pit of materialism. They begin at a point which the previous generation did not believe to exist—a visible world reduced by positive science to the invisible world of philosophy. They confront not a quantitative universe, but a qualitative. They almost begin at the very spirit of man ; they cannot advance far before they find themselves groping in the unseen, and using, not the senses given to us by action, but the eyes and ears of the understanding, by which alone the soul of man can apprehend reality. Even the Germans have gone back to Goethe.

This, then, is the contribution which Dr. Jacks makes to modern thought. We are to consider man as a creature of boundless potentiality, to realise that his first need is for light, and to define that mystic all-important word in terms of education. Christianity was not concerned with the moral law ; it was concerned with the transcending of all law by the spirit of understanding.

I need not guard myself against the supposition that so true a scholar is satisfied with the system of education which exists at the present time. Dr. Jacks looks for a reform of this system, but not from the present race of politicians.

" How can we hope to get a true system of education from politics ? " he asked me. " Is there any atmosphere more degrading ? Plato has warned us that no man is fit to govern until he has ceased to desire power. But these men think of nothing else. To be in power ; that is the game of politics. What can you expect from such people ? "

He said to me, " Men outside politics are beginning to see what education involves. It involves the whole man, body, mind, spirit. I do not think you can frame an intelligent definition of education without coming up against religion. In its simplest expression, education is a desire to escape from darkness into light. It is fear of ignorance, and faith in knowledge. At the present time, most people have escaped from darkness into twilight ; a twilight which is neither one thing nor the other. But they will never rest there. The quest of the human spirit is Goethe's dying cry, Light—more Light. And it is from these men that I look to get a nobler system of education. They will compel the politicians to act, perhaps get rid of the present race of politicians altogether And when these humble disciples of knowledge, who are now making heroic efforts to escape from the darkness of ignorance, frame their definition of education, I am sure it will include religion. The Spirit of Man needs only to be liberated to recognise the Spirit of God."

Most people, I think, will agree with Dr. Jacks in these opinions ; they are intelligent and promise a reasonable way out of our present chaos. For many they will shed a new light on their old ideas of both religion and education. But some will ask : What is the Unitarian Church doing to make these intelligent opinions prevail ?

Dr. Jacks confesses to me that there is no zeal of propaganda in the Unitarian communion. It is a society of people which does not thrust itself upon the notice of men, does not compete for converts with other churches in the market-place. It is rather a little temple of peace round the corner, to which people, who are aweary of the din in the theological market-place, may make their way if they choose. It is such a Church as Warburton, to the great joy of Edward FitzGerald, likened to Noah's family in the Ark :

> The Church, like the Ark of Noah, is worth saving ; not for the sake of the unclean beasts that almost filled it and probably made most noise and clamour in it, but for the little corner of rationality that was as much distressed by the stink within as by the tempest without.

It is significant of the modesty of the Unitarian that he does not emerge from this retirement even to cry, " I told you so," to a Church which is coming more and more to accept the simplicity of his once ridiculed and anathematised theology.

" You must regard modernism," I said to Dr. Jacks on one occasion, " as a vindication of the Unitarian attitude."

He smiled and made answer, " Better not say so. Let them follow their own line."

No man was ever less of a proselytiser. In his remarkable book *From Authority to Freedom*, in which he tells the story of Charles Hargrove's religious pilgrimage, he seems to be standing aside from all human intervention, watching with patient eyes the action of the Spirit of God on the hearts and consciences of men. And in that little master-piece of deep thought and beautiful writing, *The Lost Radiance of the Christian Religion*, from which I have made most of the quotations in this chapter, one is conscious throughout of a strong aversion from the field of dogma and controversy, a deliberate determination of the writer to keep himself in the pure region of the spirit.

Christianity, he tells us there, has seen many corruptions, but the most serious of all is not to be found in any list of doctrines that have gone wrong :

> We find it rather in a change of atmosphere, in a loss of brightness and radiant energy, in a tendency to revert in spirit, if not in terminology, to much colder conceptions of God, of man, and of the universe.

" As man in his innermost nature is a far higher

being than he seems, so the world in its innermost nature is a far nobler fabric than it seems." To discover this man must live in his spirit.

"God," said Jesus, "is Spirit," and it is a definition of God which goes behind and beneath all the other names that are applied to Him. . . .

The spirit is love ; it is peace ; it is joy ; and perhaps joy most of all. It is a joyous energy, having a centre in the soul of man.

It is not a foreign principle which has to be introduced into a man from without ; it belongs to the substance and structure of his nature ; it needs only to be liberated there ; and when once that is done it takes possession of all the forces of his being, repressing nothing, but transfiguring everything, till all his motives and desires are akindle and aglow with the fires and energy of that central flame, with its love, its peace, its joy.

A man who sees so deeply into the truth of things, and lives so habitually at the centre of existence, is not likely to display the characteristics of the propagandist. But the work of Dr. Jacks at Manchester College may yet give not only this country but the world—for his students come from many nations—a little band of radiant missionaries whose message will repel none and attract many.

Chapter V

BISHOP HENSLEY HENSON

He early attained a high development, but he has not increased it since ; years have come, but they have whispered little ; as was said of the second Pitt, " He never grew, he was cast."—WALTER BAGEHOT.

RUMOUR has it that Dr. Henson is beginning to draw in his horns. Every curate who finds himself unable to believe in the Virgin Birth, so it is said, feels himself entitled to a living in the diocese of Durham. They flee from the intolerant zealotry of the sacerdotal south to the genial modernism of the latitudinarian north.

But the trouble is, so rumour has it, these intelligent curates prove themselves but indifferent parish priests. Dr. Henson has to complain. The work of the Church must be carried on. Evangelicalism seems a better driving force than theology. Dr. Henson has to think whether perhaps . .

One need not stop to ask if this version is strictly true   The fact seems to emerge that the Bishop of Durham, one of the ablest intellects in the Church of England, and hitherto one of the strongest pillars of modernism, is beginning to speak theologically with rather less decision

86

Let us at least express the pious hope that the Dean of Durham, Dr. Welldon, has had nothing to do with it.

A greater man than Dr. Henson, a greater scholar and a profounder thinker, has spoken to me of this new movement in the Bishop's mind with a deep impersonal regret. Modernism will go on ; but what will happen to Dr. Henson ? " A man may change his mind once," he said ; " but to change it twice——"

The words of Guicciardini came into my mind " The most fatal of all neutralities is that which results not from choice, but from irresolution."

There is much to be learned, I think, from a study of Dr. Henson's personality. He stands for the moment at a parting of the ways, and it will be interesting to see which road he intends to take ; but the major interest lies in his abiding psychology, and no change in theological opinions will affect that psychology at all. Attach to him the label of " modernist " or the label of " traditionalist." and it will still be the same little eager man thrusting his way forward on either road with downward head and peering eyes, arguing with anyone who gets in his way, and loving his argument far more than his way.

When he was at Oxford, and was often in controversial conflict with Dr. A. C. Headlam, now Regius Professor of Divinity, Dr. Hensley Henson earned the nickname of Coxley Cocksure. Never was any man more certain he was right ; never was any man more inclined to ridicule the bare idea that his opponent could be anything but wrong ; and never was any man more thoroughly happy in making use of a singularly trenchant intellect to stab and thrust its triumphant way through the logic of his adversary.

It is said that Dr. Henson has had to fight his way into notice, and that he has never lost the defect of those qualities which enabled him so victoriously to reach the mitred top of the ecclesiastical tree. He has climbed. He has loved climbing. Perhaps he has so got into this bracing habit that he may even " climb down," if only in order once more to ascend—a new rendering of *reculer pour mieux sauter.* I do not think he has much altered since he first set out to conquer fortune by the force of his intellect, an intellect of whose great qualities he has always been perhaps a little dangerously self-conscious.

Few men are more effective in soliloquy. It is a memorable sight to see him standing with his back to one of the high stone mantelpieces in Durham Castle, his feet wide apart on the hearth-rug, his hands in the openings of his apron, his trim and dapper body swaying ceaselessly from the waist, his head, with its smooth boyish hair, bending constantly forward, jerking every now and then to emphasise a point in his argument, the light in his bright, watchful, sometimes mischievous eyes dancing to the joy of his own voice, the thin lips working with pleasure as they give to all his words the fullest possible value of vowels and sibilants, the small greyish face, with its two slightly protruding teeth on the lower lip, almost quivering, almost glowing, with the rhythm of his sentences and the orderly sequence of his logic. All this composes a picture which one does not easily forget. It is like the harangue of a snake, which is more subtle than any beast of the field. One is conscious of a spell.

The dark tapestried room, the carved ceiling, the heavy furniture, the embrasured windows, the whole sombre magnificence of the historic setting, quiet, almost somnolent, with the enduring memories of Cuthbert Tunstall and Butler, Lightfoot and Westcott, add a most telling vivacity to the slim and dominating figure of this boylike bishop, who is so athletic in the use of his intellect and so happy in every thesis he sets himself to establish.

It is an equally memorable sight to see him in his castle at Bishop Auckland in the rôle of host, entertaining people of intelligence with the history of the place, showing the pictures and the chapel, exhibiting curious relics of the past—a restless and energetic figure, holding its own in effectiveness against men of greater stature and more commanding presence by an inward force which has something of the tang of a twitching bowstring.

So much energy would suggest a source of almost inexhaustible power. But that is perhaps the greatest disappointment of all in the Bishop's psychology. In the case of Dr. Inge one is very conscious of a rich and deep background, a background of mysticism, from which the intellect emerges with slow emphasis to play its part on the world's stage. In the case of Bishop Ryle one is conscious behind the pleasant, courtierlike, and

scholarly manner of a background of very wholesome and unquestioning moral earnestness. But
in Dr. Henson one is conscious of nothing behind
the intellect but intellect itself, an intellect which
has absorbed his spiritual life into itself and will
permit no other tenant of his mind to divert attention for a single moment from its luminous brilliance,
its perfection of mechanism.

One may be quite wrong, of course; one can
speak only of the impression which he makes upon
oneself and perhaps a few of one's friends; but it
would almost seem as if he had ever regarded
Christianity as a thesis to be argued, not a religion
to be preached, a principle to be enunciated, not a
practice to be extended, a tradition to be maintained,
not a passion to be communicated.

Yet his sermons, which a great Anglo-Catholic
declared to me with a mocking mordancy to be
full of " edification," do often enter that region
of religion which seems to demand an appeal to
the emotions; moreover, it is not to be thought for
a moment that the Bishop is not deeply concerned
with all moral questions, that he is in the least
degree indifferent to the high importance of conduct.
But for myself these excursions, earnest and well-
intentioned as they are, proclaim rather the social
energy of the good citizen than the fervent zeal of
an apostle on fire with his Master's message. The
evangelicalism of the Bishop has taken, as it were,
the cast of politics, and he enters the pulpit of
Christ to proclaim the reasonableness of the moral
law with the alacrity of the lecturer.

This is what makes him so interesting a study

for those curious about the workings of religious psychology. Here is a thoroughly good man, as fearless and upright as any man in the kingdom, a figure among scholars, a power among organisers, a very able, sincere, and trenchant personality, who has thrown the whole weight of all he has to give on the side of Christianity, but who, for some reason, in despite of all his hard work and unquestionable earnestness, does not convey any idea of the attraction of Christ.

It makes one doubt, not that the Bishop has reserved his feelings for another affection, but whether he has any feelings to bestow. One thinks that he has drawn up and concentrated so effectually all the forces of his personality into the intellect that it is now impossible for him to see religion except as an intellectual problem. One thinks, too, that he has never dreamed of converting other people to his views, but only of arguing them out of theirs. Yet, after all, there are more ways of converting the world than beating a drum.

I am certain, however, that he could easier convince a socialistic collier or a communistic iron-moulder of the absurdity of his economics than persuade either the one or the other of the spiritual satisfaction of his own religion. Perhaps religion presents itself to the Bishop, as it does to a great number of other people, as a consecration of moral law, and clearly moral law is something to be established by reason, not commended by appeals to the sentiments ; not for one moment, all the same, would he countenance the famous cynicism of Gibbon—" The various modes of worship, which prevailed in the Roman world, were all considered by the people as equally true ; by the philosophers as equally false ; and by the magistrate as equally useful "—for no man sees more clearly the permanent need of religion in the human spirit, and no man is more sincerely convinced of the truth of the Christian religion. But he brings to religion, as I think, only his intellect, and so he has intellectualised its ethic, and has left its deepest meaning to those who possess, what he has either always lacked or has forfeited in his intellectual discipleship, the qualities of mysticism.

One might almost say that he has intellectualised the Sermon on the Mount, dissected the Prodigal Son as a study in psychology, and taken the heart out of the Fourth Gospel.

His usefulness, however, is of a high order. With the sole exception of Dean Inge, no front bench Churchman has displayed a more admirable courage in confronting democracy and challenging its materialistic politics. Moreover, although he modestly doubts his effectiveness as a public speaker, he has shown an acute judgment in these attacks which has not been lost upon the steadier minds in the Labour world of the north. Perhaps he has done as much as any man up there to convince an embittered and disillusioned proletariat that it must accept the inevitable rulings of economic law.

His courage in this matter is all the more praiseworthy because he seems to be convinced, to speak in general terms, that the religion of Christ is now rejected by the democracy. It needs, therefore, great strength of mind to face a body of men who have lost all interest in his religion, and to address them not only as economist and historian but as one who still believes that Christianity bestows a power which sets at defiance all the worst that circumstance and condition can do to the soul of man.

In these addresses he puts aside the materialistic dreams of the social reformer as impractical and dangerous.

> Ideal reconstructions of society, pictures of " The Kingdom of God upon earth," to use a popular but perilous phrase, are not greatly serviceable to human progress. They may even turn men aside from the road of actual progress, for the indulgence of philanthropic imagination neither strengthens the will in self-sacrifice, nor illumines the practical judgment.

His argument then leads him to question the justification of the social reformer's oratory "Let us be on our guard," he says, "against exaggeration."

> I am sure that great harm is being done at the present time by the reckless denunciation of the existing social order, often by men who have no special knowledge either of the history of society, or of the present situation. Hypnotised by their own enthusiasm, they allow themselves to use language which is not only altogether excessive, but also highly inflammatory. I am bound honestly to say that I think some of the clergy are great offenders in this respect. Having created or stimulated popular discontent by such rhetorical exaggeration, they point to the discontent as itself sufficient proof of the

existence of social oppression. They are immersed in a fallacy.

With boldness he carries the war into the camp of his enemies :

> There is much food for thought in the notorious fact that the critics of existing society, so far from being able to count upon the popular discontent, are compelled to organise an elaborate system of defaming propaganda in order to induce the multitude to believe themselves oppressed.

He charges the social reformer with an immoral idealism. The worker is encouraged to prolong his work, is taught that he may with perfect justice adopt the policy of ca' canny, seeing that his first duty is, not to his master, but to his wife and children.

" Imagine the effect on character," cries the Bishop, " of eight hours' dishonesty every day, eight hours of a man's second or third best, never his whole heart in his job ! And this is called idealism ! "

> If industrialism were swept away, and some form of Socialism were established, the success of the new order, as of the old, would have to turn on the willingness of the people honestly to work it. It hardly lies in the mouths of men who are labouring incessantly to obstruct the working of the existing order, to build an argument against it on the measure of their success in making it fail. There are confessedly many grave evils in our industrial system, but there are also very evident benefits. It is, like human nature itself, a mingled thing. Instead of exaggerating the evils, the wiser course would surely be to inquire how far

they are capable of remedy, and then cautiously—for the daily bread of these many millions of British folk depends on the normal working of our industrial system—to attempt reforms.   Reckless denunciation is not only wrong in itself, but it creates a listless, disaffected temper, the farthest removed possible from the spirit of good citizenship and honest labour.

In these quotations you may see something of the Bishop's acuteness of intellect, something of his courage, and something of his wholesome good sense. But, also, I venture to think, one may see in them something of his spiritual limitations.

For, after all, is not the Christian challenged with an identical criticism by the champions of materialism ?

Why can't he leave people alone ?   Who asks him to interfere with the lives of other people—other people who are perfectly contented to go their own way ?   Look at the rascal !   Having created or stimulated spiritual discontent by rhetorical exaggeration, he points to the discontent as itself sufficient proof of the dissatisfaction of materialism !   Out upon him, for a paid agitator, a kill-joy, and a humbug.   Let him hold his peace, or, with Nietzsche, consign these masses of the people " to the Devil and the Statistician."

Might it not be argued that the Bishop's attitude towards the social reformer bears at least a slight family resemblance to the attitude of the Pharisees towards Christ, and of the Roman Power to the earliest Christian communities ?   May it not be said, too, that nothing is so disagreeable to a conservative mind as the fermentation induced by the leaven of a new idea?

Never does dissatisfaction with the present condition of things appear in the Bishop's eyes as a creation of the Christian spirit, an extension of that liberalising, enfranchising, and enriching spirit which has already destroyed so many of the works of feudalism. But he faces the question of the part which the Church must play in the world; he faces it with honesty and answers it with shrewdness—

> What then is the rôle of the Church in such a world as this? Surely it is still what it was before—to be the soul of society, " the salt of the earth." If we, Christ's people, are carrying on, year in and year out, a quiet, persistent witness by word and life to " the things that are more excellent," the unseen things which are eternal, we too shall be " holding the world together," and opening before society the vista of a genuine progress. This is the supreme and incommunicable task of the Church; this is the priceless service which we can render to the nation.

The position is defensible, for it is one that has been held by the saints, and dangerous indeed is the spirit of materialism in the region of social reform. But does not one miss from the Bishop's attack upon the social reformer something much deeper than successful logic, something which expresses itself in the works of other men by the language of sympathy and charity, something which hungers and thirsts to shed light and to give warmth, something which makes for the eventual brotherhood of mankind under the divine Fatherhood of God?

Some such spirit as this, I think, is to be found in the writings of Mr. R. H. Tawney, who, however much he may err and go astray in his economics, cherishes at least a more seemly vision of the human family than that which now passes for civilisation. Is it not possible that the day may come when a gigantic income will seem " ungentlemanly " ? Is it not a just claim, a Christian claim, that the social organisation should be based upon " moral principles " ?

Christians are a sect, and a small sect, in a Pagan Society. But they can be a sincere sect. If they are sincere, they will not abuse the Pagans . . . for a good Pagan is an admirable person. But he is not a Christian, for his hopes and fears, his preferences and dislikes, his standards of success and failure, are different from those of Christians. The Church will not pretend that he is, or endeavour to make its own Faith acceptable to him by diluting the distinctive ethical attributes of Christianity till they become inoffensive, at the cost of becoming trivial.

. . . so tepid and self-regarding a creed is not a religion. Christianity cannot allow its sphere to be determined by the convenience of politicians or by the conventional ethics of the world of business. The whole world of human interests was assigned to it as its province (*The Acquisitive Society*).

It must not be supposed that the Bishop has no answer to this criticism of his attitude. He would say, " Produce your socialistic scheme, and I will examine it, and if it will work and if it is just I will support it ; but until you have found this scheme, what moral right do you possess which entitles you to unsettle men's minds, to fill their hearts with the bitterness of discontent, and to turn the attention of their souls away from the things that are more excellent ? "

On this ground, the ground of economics, his position seems to me unassailable ; but it is a position which suggests the posture of a lecturer in front of his blackboard rather than that of a shepherd seeking the lost sheep of his flock. If the socialist must think again, at least we may ask that the Bishop should sometimes raise his crook to defend the sheep against the attack of the robber and the wolf. If the sheep are to be patient, if they are not to stray, if they are not to die, there must be food for their grazing.

But the Bishop, at the very roots of his being, is conservative, and the good qualities of conservatism do not develop foresight or permit of vision. He would stick to the wattled cotes ; and I think he would move his flock on to new pastures as seldom as possible. This will not do, however. The social reformer tells the Bishop who thinks democracy has rejected religion that " the hungry sheep look up and are not fed." The roots of the old sustenance are nibbled level to the ground, and the ground itself is sour. If socialism is wrong, let the Bishop tell us where lies a safer pasture.

One seems to see in this thrusting scholar and restless energetic prelate a very striking illustration of the need in the Christian of tenderness. Intellect is not enough. Intellect, indeed, is not light ; it is only the wick of a lamp which must be fed constantly with the oil of compassion—that is to say, if its light is to shine before men. The

Bishop dazzles, but he does not illumine the darkness or throw a white beam ahead of heavy-laden and far-journeying humanity on the road which leads, let us hope, to a better order of things than the present system.

Whether such a man calls himself traditionalist or modernist does not greatly matter.   One respects him for his moral qualities, his courage, and his devotion to his work ; one honours him for his intellectual qualities, which are of a high and brilliant order ; but one does not feel that he is leading the advance, or even that he knows in which direction the army is definitely advancing.

CHAPTER VI

MISS MAUDE ROYDEN

. . . their religion, too (i.e. the religion of women), has a mode of expressing itself, though it seldom resorts to the ordinary phrases of divinity.

Those " nameless, unremembered acts of kindness and of love," by which their influence is felt through every part of society, humanising and consoling wherever it travels, are their theology. It is thus that they express the genuine religion of their minds ; and we trust that if ever they should study the ordinary dialect of systematised religion they will never, while pronouncing its harsh gutterals and stammering over its difficult shibboleths, forget their elder and simpler and richer and sweeter language.—F. D. MAURICE.

PUSHKIN said that Russia turned an Asian face towards Europe and a European face towards Asia.

This acute saying may be applied to Miss Royden. To the prosperous and timid Christian she appears as a dangerous evangelist of socialism, and to the fiery socialist as a tame and sentimental apostle of Christianity. As in the case of Russia, so in the case of this interesting and courageous woman ; one must go to neither extremity, neither to the *bourgeoisie* nor to the *apacherie*, if one would discover the truth of her nature.

Nor need one fear to go direct to the lady herself, for she is the very soul of candour. Moreover, she has that charming spirit of friendliness and communication which distinguished La Bruyère, a philosopher " always accessible, even in his deepest studies, who tells you to come in, for you bring him something more precious than gold or silver, *if it is the opportunity of obliging you.*"

Certainly Miss Royden does not resemble, in her attitude towards either God or the human race, that curious *religieuse* Mdme. de Maintenon, who having been told by her confessor in the flood-time of her beauty that " God wished her to become the King's mistress," at the end of that devout if somewhat painful experience, replied to a suggestion about writing her memoirs, " Only saints would find pleasure in its perusal."

Miss Royden's memoirs, if they are ever written, would have, I think, the rather unusual merit of pleasing both saints and sinners ; the saints by the depth and beauty of her spiritual experience, the sinners by her freedom from every shade of cant and by her strong, almost masculine, sympathy with the difficulties of our human nature. Catherine the Great, in her colloquies with the nervous and hesitating Diderot, used to say, " Proceed ; *between men* all is allowable." One may affirm of Miss Royden that she is at once a true woman and a great man.

It is this perfect balance of the masculine and feminine in her personality which makes her so effective a public speaker, so powerful an influence in private discourse, and so safe a writer on questions of extreme delicacy, such as the problem of sex. She is always on the level of the whole body of humanity, a complete person, a veritable human being, neither a member of a class nor the representative of a sex.

Perhaps it may be permitted to mention two events in her life which help one to understand how it is she has come to play this masculine and feminine part in public life.

One day, a day of torrential rain, when she was a girl living in her father's house in Cheshire, she and her sister saw a carriage and pair coming through the park towards the house. The coachman and footman on the box were soaking wet, and kept their heads down to avoid the sting of the rain in their eyes. The horses were streaming with rain and the carriage might have been a water-cart.

When the caller, a rich lady, arrived in the drawing-room, polite wonder was expressed at her boldness in coming out on such a dreadful day. She seemed surprised. " Oh, but I came in a closed carriage," she explained.

This innocent remark opened the eyes of Miss Royden to the obliquity of vision which is wrought, all unconsciously in many cases, by the power of selfishness. The condition of her coachman and footman had never for a moment presented itself to the lady's mind. Miss Royden made acquaintance with righteous indignation. She became a reformer, and something of a vehement reformer.

The drenched carriage coming through a splash of rain to her home will remain for ever in her mind as an image of that spirit of selfishness which in its manifold and subtle workings wrecks the beauty of human existence.

Miss Royden, it should be said, had been prepared by a long experience of pain to feel sympathy with the sufferings of other people. Her mind had been lamentably ploughed up ever since the dawn of memory to receive the divine grain of compassion.

At birth both her hips were dislocated, and lameness has been her lot through life. Such was her spirit, however, that this saddening and serious affliction, dogging her days and nights with pain, seldom prevented her from joining in the vigorous games and sports of the Royden family. She was something of a boy even in those days, and pluck was the very centre of her science of existence.

The religion of her parents suggested to her mind that this suffering had been sent by God. She accepted the perilous suggestion, but never confronted it. It neither puffed her up with spiritual pride nor created in her mind bitter thoughts of a paltry and detestable Deity. A pagan stoicism helped her to bear her lot quite as much as, if not more than, the evangelicalism of Sir Thomas and Lady Royden. Moreover, she was too much in love with life to give her mind very seriously to the difficulties of theology. Even with a body which had to wrench itself along, one could swim and row, read and think, observe and worship.

Her eldest brother went to Winchester and Magdalen College at Oxford; she to Cheltenham College and Lady Margaret Hall at Oxford.

Education was an enthusiasm. Rivalry in scholarship was as greatly a part of that wholesome family
life as rivalry in games. There was always a
Socratic " throwing of the ball " going on, both
indoors and out. Miss Royden distinguished herself
in the sphere of learning and in the sphere of sports.

At Oxford the last vestiges of her religion, or
rather her parents' religion, faded from her mind,
without pain of any order, hardly with any consciousness. She devoted herself wholeheartedly to the
schools. No longer did she imagine that God
had sent her lameness. She ceased to think of
Him.

But one day she heard a sermon which made
her think of Jesus as a teacher, just as one thinks
of Plato and Aristotle. She reflected that she
really knew more of the teaching of Plato and
Aristotle than she knew of Christ's teaching. This
seemed to her an unsatisfactory state of things,
and she set herself, as a student of philosophy, to
study the teaching of Jesus. What had He said ?
Never mind whether He had founded this Church
or that, what had He said ? And what had been
His science of life, His reading of the riddle ?

This study, to which she brought a philosophic
mind and a candid heart, convinced her that the
teaching should be tried. It was, indeed, a teaching that asked men to prove it by trial. She
decided to try it, and she tried it by reading, by
meditation, and by prayer. The trial was a failure.
But in this failure was a mystery. For the more
she failed the more profoundly conscious she became
of Christ as a Power. This feeling remained with

her, and it grew stronger with time. The Christ
who would not help her nevertheless tarried as a
shadow haunting the background of her thoughts.

There was a secret in life which she had missed,
a power which she had never used. Then came the
second event to which I have referred. Miss Royden
met a lady who had left the Church of England
and joined the Quakers, seeking by this change to
intensify her spiritual experience, seeking to make
faith a deep personal reality in her life. This lady
told Miss Royden the following experience :

One day, at a Quakers' meeting, she had earnestly
" besieged the Throne of Grace" during the silence
of prayer, imploring God to manifest Himself to
her spirit. So earnestly did she " besiege the
Throne of Grace " in this silent intercession of soul
that at last she was physically exhausted and
could frame no further words of entreaty. At
that moment she heard a voice in her soul, and
this voice said to her, " Yes, I have something to
say to you, *when you stop your shouting.*"

From this experience Miss Royden learned to
see the tremendous difference between physical
and spiritual silence. She cultivated, with the
peace of soul which is the atmosphere of surrender
and dependence, silence of spirit ; and out of this
silence came a faith against which the gates of hell
could not prevail ; and out of that faith, winged
by her earliest sympathy with all suffering and all
sorrow, came a desire to give herself up to the
service of God. She had found the secret, she could
use the power.

Her first step towards a life of service was

joining a Women's Settlement in Liverpool, a city which has wealth enough to impress and gratify the disciples of Mr. Samuel Smiles, and slums enough to excite and infuriate the disciples of Karl Marx. Here Miss Royden worked for three years, serving her novitiate as it were in the ministry of mercy, a notable figure in the dark streets of Liverpool, that little eager body, with its dragging leg, its struggling hips, its head held high to look the whole world in the face on the chance, nay, but in the hope, that a bright smile from eyes as clear as day might do some poor devil a bit of good.

She brought to the slums of Liverpool the gay cheerfulness of a University woman, Oxford's particular brand of cheerfulness, and also a tenderness of sympathy and a graciousness of helpfulness which was the fine flower of deep, inward, silent, personal religion.

It is not easy for anyone with profound sympathy to believe that individual Partingtons can sweep back with their little mops of beneficence and philanthropy the Atlantic Ocean of sin, suffering, and despair which floods in to the shores of our industrialism—at high tide nearly swamping its prosperity, and at low tide leaving all its ugliness, squalor, and despairing hopelessness bare to the eye of heaven.

Miss Royden looked out for something with a wider sweep, and in the year 1908 joined the Women's Suffrage Movement. It was her hope, her conviction, that woman's influence in politics might have a cleansing effect in the national life. She became an advocate of this great Movement, but an advocate who always based her argument on religious grounds. She had no delusions about materialistic politics. Her whole effort was to spiritualise the public life of England.

Here she made a discovery—a discovery of great moment to her subsequent career. She discovered that many came to her meetings, and sought personal interviews or written correspondence with her afterwards, who were not greatly interested in the franchise, but who were interested, in some tragic cases poignantly interested, in spiritual enfranchisement. Life revealed itself to her as a struggle between the higher and lower nature, a conflict in the will between good and evil. She was at the heart of evolution.

It became evident to Miss Royden that she had discovered for herself both a constituency and a church. Some years after making this discovery she abandoned all other work, and ever since, first at the City Temple and now at the Guildhouse in Eccleston Square, has been one of the most effective advocates in this country of personal religion.

She does not impress one by the force of her intellect, but rather by the force of her humanity. You take it for granted that she is a scholar ; you are aware of her intellectual gifts, I mean, only as you are aware of her breeding. The main impression she makes is one of full humanity, humanity at its best, humanity that is pure but not self-righteous, charitable but not sentimental, just but not hard, true but not mechanical in consistency, frank but not gushing. Out of all this come two things, the sense of two realisms, the realism of her political

faith, and the realism of her religious faith. You
are aware that she feels the sufferings and the
deprivations of the oppressed in her own blood, and
feels the power, the presence, and the divinity of
Christ in her own soul.

It is a grateful experience to sit with this woman,
who is so like the best of men but is so manifestly
the staunchest of women. Her face reveals the
force of her emotions, her voice, which is musical
and persuasive, the depth of her compassion. In
her sitting-room, which is almost a study and nearly
an office, hangs a portrait of Newman, and a *prie-
Dieu* stands against one of the walls half-hidden by
bookshelves. She is one of the few very busy people
I have known who give one no feeling of an inward
commotion.

Apart from her natural eloquence and her unmis-
takable sincerity, apart even from the attractive
fullness of her humanity, I think the notable success
of her preaching is to be attributed to a single
reason, quite outside any such considerations. It
is a reason of great importance to the modern
student of religious psychology. Miss Royden
preaches Christ as a Power.

To others she leaves the esoteric aspects of religion,
and the ceremonial of worship, and the difficulties
of theology, and the mechanism of parochial organisation. Her mission, as she receives it, is to preach
to people who are unwilling and suffering victims
of sin, or who are tortured by theological indecision,
that Christ is a Power, a Power that works miracles,
a Power that can change the habits of a lifetime,
perhaps the very tissues of a poisoned body, and

can give both peace and guidance to the soul that is dragged this way and that.

One may be pardoned for remarking that this is a rather unusual form of preaching in any of the respectable churches. Christianity as a unique power in the world, a power which transfigures human life, which tears habitude up by the roots, and which gives new strength to the will, new eyes to the soul, and a new reality to the understanding; this, strange to say, is an unusual, perhaps an unpopular subject of clerical discourse. It is Miss Royden's insistent contribution to modern theology.

She tells me that so far as her own experience goes, humanity does not seem to be troubled by intellectual doubts. She is inclined to think that it is even sick of such discussions, and is apt to describe them roughly and impatiently as " mere talk." Humanity, as she sees it, is immersed in the incessant struggle of moral evolution.

There is an empiricism of religion which is worth attention. It challenges the sceptic to explain both the conversion of the sinner and the beauty of the saint. If religion can change a man's whole character in the twinkling of an eye, if it can give a beauty of holiness to human nature such as is felt by all men to be the highest expression of man's spirit, truly it is a science of life which works, and one which its critics must explain. The theories of dogmatist and traditionalist are not the authentic documents of the Christian religion. Let the sceptic bring his indictment against the changed lives of those who attribute to Christ alone the daily miracle of their gladness.

What men and women want to know in these days, Miss Royden assures me out of the richness of her great experience, is whether Christianity works, *whether it does things*. The majority of people, she feels sure, are looking about for " something that helps "—something that will strengthen men and women to fight down their lower nature, that will convince them that their higher nature is a reality, and that will give them a living sense of companionship in their difficult lives—lives often as drab and depressing as they are morally difficult.

Because she can convey this great sense of the power of Christianity, people all over the country go to hear her preach and lecture. She is, I think, one of the most persuasive preachers of the power of Christianity in any English-speaking country. It is impossible to feel of her that she is merely speaking of something she has read about in books, or of something which she recommends because it is apostolic and traditional ; she brings home to the mind of the most cynical and ironical that her message, so modestly and gently given, is nevertheless torn out of her inmost soul by a deep inward experience and by a sympathy with humanity which altogether transfigures her simple words.

It must be difficult, I should think, for any fair-minded sceptic not to give this religion at least a practical trial after hearing Miss Royden's exposition of it and after learning from her the manner in which that experiment should be carried out. For she speaks as one having the authority of a deep personal experience, making no dogmatic claims, expressing sympathy with all those who fail, but assuring her hearers that when the moment comes for their illumination it will come, and that it will be a veritable dayspring from on high. Earnestness is hers of the highest and tenderest order, but also the convincing authority of one who has found the peace which passes understanding.

She has spoken to me with sympathy of Mr. Studdert-Kennedy, whose trench-like methods in the pulpit are thoroughly distasteful to a great number of people. It is characteristic of Miss Royden that she should fasten on the real cause of this violence. " I don't like jargon," she said, " particularly the jargon of Christian Science and Theosophy. I love English literature too much for that ; and I don't like slang, particularly slang of a brutal order ; but I feel a deep sympathy with anybody who is trying, as Mr. Studdert-Kennedy is trying, to put life and power into institutionalism. It wants it so badly—oh, so very badly—life, life, life and power."

Of one whose scholarship greatly impresses her, and for whose spiritual life she has true respect, but whose theology fills her soul with dark shadows and cold shudders, she exclaimed, as though it were her own fault for not understanding him, " It is as if God were dead ! "

Always she wants Christianity as life and power.

She remains a social reformer, and is disposed to agree with Bishop Gore that the present system is so iniquitous that it cannot be Christianised. She thinks it must be destroyed, but admits the peril of destructive work till a new system is ready to take its place.

Yet I feel fairly certain that she would admit, if pressed with the question, that the working of any better system can depend for its success only upon a much better humanity. For she is one of those who is bewildered by the selfishness of men and women, a brutal, arrogant, challenging, and wholly unashamed selfishness, which publicly seeks its own pleasures, publicly displays the offending symbols of its offensive wealth, publicly indulges itself in most shameful and infuriating luxuries, even at a time when children are dying like flies of starvation and pestilence, and while the men of their own household, who fought to save civilisation from the despotism of the Prussian theory, tramp the streets, hungry and bitter-hearted, looking for work.

On her mind, moving about England at all times of the year, the reality of these things is for ever pressing ; the unthinkable selfishness of so many, and the awful depression of the multitude. She says that a system which produces, or permits, such a state of things must be bad, and radically bad.

There are moments, when she speaks of these things, which reveal to one a certain anger of her soul, a disposition, if I may say so with great respect, towards vehemence, a temper of impatience and indignation which would surely have carried her into the camp of anarchy but for the restraining power of her religious experience. She feels, deeply and burningly, but she has a Master. The flash comes into her eyes, but the habitual serenity returns.

I think, however, she might be persuaded to

believe that it is not so much the present system but the pagan selfishness of mankind which brings these unequal and dreadful things to pass. The lady in the closed carriage would not be profoundly changed, we may suppose, by a different system of economics, but surely she might be changed altogether—body, soul, and spirit—if she so willed it, by that Power which has directed Miss Royden's own life to such beautiful and wonderful ends.

Nevertheless, Miss Royden must be numbered among the socialists, the Christian socialists, and Individualism will be all the better for asking itself how it is that a lady so good, so gentle, so clear-headed, and so honest should be arrayed with its enemies.

I should like to speak of one memorable experience in Miss Royden's later life.

She has formed a little, modest, unknown, and I think nameless guild for personal religion. She desires that nothing of its work should get into the press and that it should not add to its numbers. She wishes it to remain a sacred confraternity of her private life, as it were the lady chapel of her cathedral services to mankind, or as a retreat for her exhausted soul.

Some months ago she asked a clergyman who has succeeded in turning into a house of living prayer a London church which before his coming was like a tomb, whether he would allow the members of this guild, all of whom are not members of the Church of England, to come to the Eucharist. He received this request with the most generous sympathy, saying that he would give them a private celebration, and one morning, soon after dawn, the guild met in this church to make its first communion. No one else was present.

Miss Royden has told me that it was an unforgettable experience. Here was a man, she said, who has no reputation as a great scholar, and no popularity as an orator ; he is loved simply for his devotion to Christ and his sympathy with the sorrows of mankind. Yet that man, as no other man had done before, brought the Presence of God into the hearts of that little kneeling guild. It was as if, Miss Royden tells me, God was there at the altar, shining upon them and blessing them. Never before had she been more certain of God as a Person.

It is from experiences of this nature that she draws fresh power to make men and women believe that the Christian religion is a true philosophy of reality, and a true science of healing. She is, I mean, a mystic. But she differs from a mystic like Dean Inge in this, that she is a mystic impelled by human sympathy to use her mysticism as her sole evangel.

CHAPTER VII

CANON E. W. BARNES

*True religion takes up that place in the mind which
superstition would usurp, and so leaves little room for it ;
and likewise lays us under the strongest obligations to
oppose it.*—BISHOP BUTLER.

*Socrates looked up at him, and replied, Farewell : I will
do as you say. Then he turned to us and said, How
courteous the man is !*—PLATO.

IN this able and courageous Doctor of Science,
who came to theology from mathematics, a great
virtue and a small fault combine to check his
intellectual usefulness. His heart is as full of
modesty as his mind of tentatives.

He is possessed by a gracious nature, and could
no more think of raising his voice to shout down
a Boanerges than he could dream of lifting an
elbow to push his way through a press of people
bound for the limelight. It is only a deep moral
earnestness which brings him into public life at all,
and he endeavours to treat that public life not as
it is but as it ought to be.

In " the calmness and moderation of his sentiments," in his dislike of everything that is sensational, and of all " undue emphasis," he resembles

Joubert, who wanted " to infuse exquisite sense
into common sense, or to render exquisite sense
common."

Modesty might not so hamper the usefulness of
Canon Barnes if he knew a little less than he does
know, and was also conveniently blind to the
vastness of scientific territory. But he knows
much ; much too much for vociferation ; and his
eyes are so wide open to the enormous sweep of
scientific inquiry that he can nowhere discern at
present the ground for a single thesis which
effectually accounts for everything—a great lack
in a popular preacher.

I am disposed to deplore the degree both of his
modesty and his scholarship, for he possesses one
of the rarest and most precious of gifts in a very
learned man, particularly a mathematician and a
theologian, namely, the gift of lucid exposition.
Few men of our day, in my judgment, are better
qualified to state the whole case for Christianity
than this distinguished Canon of Westminster
Abbey, this evangelical Fellow of the Royal
Society, who is nevertheless prevented from attracting the attention of the multitude by the
gracious humility of his nature and the intellectual
nervousness which is apt to inhibit his free
utterance when he approaches an audience in the
region of science.

What a pity that a clergyman so charming and
attractive, and yet so modern, who understands the
relativity of Einstein and who is admirably grounded
in the physical sciences, should lack that fighting
instinct, that " confidence of reason," which in

Father Waggett, an equally charming person, caught the attention of the religious world thirty or forty years ago.

His mind is not unlike the mind of Lord Robert Cecil, and it is curious that even physically he should at certain moments resemble Lord Robert, particularly in his walk and the almost set expression of his eyes. He is tall and thin, and has the same stoop in the shoulders, moving forward as if an invisible hand were pressed against the back of his neck, shoving him forward by a series of jerks ; and he seems to throw, like Lord Robert, a particular sense of enjoyment into the motion of his legs, as though he would get rid of all perilous swagger at that, the less harmful end of his two extremities—the antipodes of his reason. Like Lord Robert, too, he has a most pleasant voice, and a slow deliberate way of speaking, and a warm kindly smile which fades at the first movement of serious thought, leaving the whole pale face, even the dark eyes under their heavy brows, almost deathlike in immobility. One seems to see in such moments the spirit withdraw from the surface of things to take up its duty at the citadel of the intellect.

The same conflict between temperament and purpose which has prevented Lord Robert Cecil from taking his place at the head of a Government prevents Canon Barnes from advancing at the head of modern Churchmen to the rich future of a depaganised and wholly rational Christianity. His heart says " Fight," but his reason says " Watch." Fighting is distasteful ; watching is congenial. Besides, while one is watching one can review all the hypotheses. A man who is not careful in destroying a fallacy may damage a truth.

But let us be grateful for his public utterances, which show a high spirit, a noble devotion, an enviable range of culture, and, for the discerning at least, tell the true time of day. It is one of the encouraging signs of the period that such distinguished preaching should have made a mark. Moreover, he is yet three years from fifty, with a mind so hospitable to growth that it has no room for one of those prejudices which are the dry-nurses of old age. Those who love truth die young, whatever their age. Canon Barnes may yet give the Church a proof of his power to lead—a Church at present aware only of his power to suggest.

He considers that we are living in a time of revolution, and, judging by historic precedents, particularly the Renaissance, he thinks we are now in the second stage of our revolution, which is the most difficult of all. First, comes the destruction of false ideas—a bracing time for the born fighter ; second, comes the tentative search for new ideas—an anxious time for the responsible philosopher ; third, comes the preaching of these new ideas with passion—the opportunity of the enthusiast. Happy were the divines of the seventeenth century !

We, however, are in the second stage.

This is not a period for new ideas : it is a period of searching for the best idea. He who rushes forward with an untried new idea may be more dangerous than he who still clings, in the Name of Christ, to an old idea which is false. We must be quite certain of our ground before we advance with boldness, and our boldness must be spiritual, not muscular.

Modernism has fought and won the battle of verbal inspiration. No man whose opinion counts in the least degree now holds that the Bible was verbally inspired by God. It is respected, honoured, loved ; but it is no longer a fetish. In ceasing to be a superstition, and in coming to be a number of genuine books full of light for the student of history, the Bible is exercising at the present time an extraordinary influence in the world, a greater influence perhaps on thoughtful minds than it ever before exercised.

The battle which modernism is now fighting over this collection of books concerns the Person of Jesus and the relative value of the gospels which narrate His life, and, in the case of the Fourth, endeavour to expound His teaching. This great battle is not over, but it looks as if victory will lie with the more moderate school of modernists. Outside very extreme circles, the old rigid notions concerning the Person of Jesus are no longer held with the passion which gave them a certain noble force in the days before Darwin. There is now a notable tell-tale petulance about orthodoxy which is sometimes insolent but never effective.

Ahead of this battle, which the present generation may live to see fought out to a conclusion, lies a third struggle likely to be of a more desperate character than its two forerunners—the battle over Sacramental Christianity. Already in France and Germany the question is asked, Did Jesus institute any sacraments at all ? But even in these two countries the battle has not yet begun in real earnest, while over here only readers of Lake and Kennedy are dimly aware of a coming storm. That storm will concern rites which few orthodox Christians have ever regarded as heathen in their spirit, though some have come to know they are pagan in origin.

It is not wise to ignore this future struggle, but our main responsibility is to bear a manful part in the struggle which is now upon us.

There are three types of modernists. There is, first of all, the Liberal, who regards Christianity as a form of Platonism resting on the idea of absolute values. This is dangerous ground : something more is required. Then there is the evangelical modernist, who accepts almost everything in the Higher Criticism, but holds to Christ as an incarnation of the Divine purpose, an incarnation, if you will, of God, all we can know of God limited by His human body, as God we must suppose is not limited, but still God. And, finally, there is the Catholic modernist, who believes in a Church, who makes the sacraments his centre of religion, and exalts Christianity to the head of all the mystery religions which have played a part in the evolution of the human race. This is not likely to be the prevailing type of modernism.

It looks as if the main body of modern opinion is moving in the direction followed by the second of these schools—the evangelical. Here is preserved all that great range of deep feeling and all that fine energy of unselfish earnestness which have given to Christianity the most effectual of its impulses. A man may still worship Christ, and still make obedience to the Will of Christ the chief passion or object of his existence, although he no longer believes that Jesus was either born out of the order of nature or died to turn away the vengeance of God from a world which had sinned itself beyond the reach of infinite love.

Like Goethe, such a man will say : " As soon as the pure doctrine and love of Christ are comprehended in their true nature, and have become a living principle, we shall feel ourselves great and free as human beings, and not attach special importance to a degree more or less in the outward forms of religion."

The critics of modernism do not seem able, for some reason, to grasp a truth which has been apparent all down the ages, a truth so old that it is almost entitled to be regarded as a tradition, and so widely held that it is almost worthy to be called catholic, namely, the truth that Jesus loses none of His power over human history so long as He abides a living principle in the hearts of individual men. So long as He expresses for mankind the Character of God and reveals to mankind the nature of God's purpose, so long as men love Him as they love no other, and set themselves to make His spirit tell, first in their lives and after that in the world about them, does it greatly matter whether they speak of His divinity or His uniqueness, whether they accept definitions concerning Him (framed by men in the dark ages) or go about to do His will with no definitions in their mind at all beyond the intellectual conviction that here is One who spoke as no other man has spoken since the creation of the world ?

Canon Barnes, who disowns the name of modernist, but who is the very opposite of an obscurantist in his evangelicalism, is careful to insist upon a *rational* loyalty to Christ. I tried one day to tempt him on this head, speaking of the miraculous changes wrought in men's lives by religious fervour pure and simple ; but it was in vain. He agrees that religious fervour may work such miracles : he is the last man in the world to dismiss these miracles as curious and interesting phenomena of psychology ; but he insists, and is like a rock on this matter, that emotional Christianity is not safe without an intellectual background.

He makes me feel that his modernism, if I may presume to use that term, is an evangelical desire of his soul to give men this intellectual background to their faith. He wants, as it were, to save their beliefs rather than their souls. He regards the emotionalist as occupying territory as dangerous to himself and to the victory of Christianity as the territory occupied by the traditionalist. Both schools offend the mind of rational men ; both make Christianity seem merely an affair of temperament ; and both are exposed to the danger of losing their faith.

To convert the world to the Will of God, it is essential that the Christian should have a rational explanation of his faith, a faith which, resting only on tradition or emotion, must obviously take its place among all the other competing religions of mankind, a religion possessing no authority recognised by the modern world.

The modern world rightly asks of every opinion

and idea presented to its judgment, " Is it true ? "
and it has reason on its side in being sceptical
concerning the records of the past. If not, there
are religions in the world of an antiquity greater
than Christianity's, whose traditions have been
faithfully kept by a vaster host of the human race
than has ever followed the traditions of Christianity.
Is it to be a battle between tradition and tradition ?
Is age to be a test of truth ?   Is devotion to a
formula to count as an argument ?

The emotionalist, too, is no longer on safe ground
in protesting his miracles of conversion. The
psychologist is advancing towards that ground,
and advancing with every theory of supernatural
evidence excluded from his mind. The psychologist
may eventually be driven to accept the Christian
explanation of these phenomena ; but until that
surrender is made the emotionalist will not be the
power in the world which he ought to be.   His house,
too, must be founded upon a rock.

Let us not be afraid of examining our faith,
bringing our minds as well as our hearts and our
souls to the place of judgment.

I will give here a few quotations from the utterances of Canon Barnes which show his position with
sufficient clearness.

We all seek for truth.   But, whereas to some truth
seems a tide destined to rise and sweep destructively
across lands where Jesus reigned as the Son of God,
to me it is the power which will set free new streams to
irrigate His Kingdom.

As is obvious to everyone, all the Churches realise,
though some do not acknowledge, the necessity of

presenting the Christian Faith in terms of current thought.

We have seen the urgent need of a fuller knowledge of the structure of the human mind if we would explain how Jesus was related to God and how we receive grace from God through Christ.

I am an Evangelical; I cannot call myself a modernist.

I have welcomed the intervention of those who, disclaiming any knowledge of scholarship or theology, have in simple language revealed the power of Christ in their lives. For theory and practice, speculation and life, cannot be separated. We cannot begin to explain Jesus until we know how men and women are transformed by the love of Christ constraining them.

Those to whom religion is external and worship formal are of necessity pretentious or arid in speaking of such matters as the Person of Christ or the value of creeds.

We do not affirm that the Lord's Person and work have been central in Christianity in the past. There is much to be said for the view that they were, from the end of the second century to the close of the Middle Ages, concealed beneath alien ideas derived from the mystery religions ; that the Reformation was the hammer which broke the husk within which, under God's providence, the kernel had been preserved during the decline and eclipse of European civilisation.

. . . as religion grows in richness and purity, Jesus comes to His own.

Reason and intuition combine to justify the belief that our Lord had a right understanding of what man can become.

We say that man is not only a part of the evolutionary process. His highest attributes must serve to show its purpose. They reveal the nature and the end of God's plan.

. . . as man develops in the way predestined by God, he will continually approach the standard set by Jesus. Jesus will ever more completely draw men and inspire them because they will more fully understand that He explains them to themselves.

The present degradation of human life is due to man's refusal to accept Christ's estimate of its values and duties. It will endure so long as the work and Person of Christ are refused their right place in human thought and aspiration.

Jesus still lives, great and unexplained.

From these quotations it will be seen that Canon Barnes is not searching the documents of Christianity for a new hypothesis, but rather for a new understanding by which he may be able to present the historic power of Christianity in terms of modern thought. Jesus remains for him the central Figure of evolution. " Human thought," he declares, " as moulded by developed aspirations and accumulated knowledge, will not sweep past Jesus but will circle round Him as the centre where God revealed Himself."

Perhaps we shall best understand the position of Canon Barnes if we see him, neither on this side nor on that of the warring controversy, but rather among the entire host of Christianity, warning all schools of thought, all parties, all sects, that they must prepare themselves for the final strife which is yet to come, that great strife, foreseen by Newman, when the two contrary principles of human life, the Good and the Evil, shall rush upon each other contending for the soul of the world. Christianity must become united and strong at its centre, if it is to withstand this onslaught.

He is not to be thought of as one who would adapt religion to the needs of the day, but as one who believes that, thoroughly understood, religion is adequate to the needs, not only of our day, but to the needs of all time. For to Canon Barnes, religion is simply the teaching of Christ, and Christ is the revelation to man of God's nature and purpose. He would simplify dogma in order to clarify truth. He would clarify truth in order to enlarge the opportunities of Christ. He would call no man a heretic who is not serving the devil. None who seeks to enter the Kingdom will ever be hindered by this devout disciple of truth in whose blood is no drop of the toxin of Pharisaism.

You may see the intellectual charity of the man in his attitude towards other teachers of our time whose views are opposed to his own. Of Dean Inge he has spoken to me with almost a ringing enthusiasm, emphasising his unbounded force, his unbounded courage ; and of Bishop Gore with the deepest respect, paying reverent tribute to his spiritual earnestness ; even the Bishop of Zanzibar provokes only a smile of the most cheerful good humour.

He inclines quietly towards optimism, believing in the providence of God and thinking that the recent indifference to religion is passing away. Men are now seeking, and to seek is eventually to find. This seeking, he observes, is among the latest utterances of theology, a fact of considerable importance. To keep abreast of truth one must neither go back nor stand still. Men are now not so much swallowing great names as looking for a candle

Not long ago he paid a visit to a favourite book-shop of his in Cambridge, and inquired for second-hand volumes of theology. " I have nothing here," replied the bookseller, " that would interest you. The books you would like go out the day after they come in, sometimes the same day." Then pointing to the upper shelves, " But I've plenty of the older books " ; and there in the dust and neglect of the top shelves Canon Barnes surveyed the works of grave and portentous theologians who wrote, some before the days of Darwin, and some in the first heyday of Darwinism. He said to me, " Light-foot is still consulted, but even Westcott is now neglected."

He spoke of two difficulties for the Church. One is this : her supreme need at the present time is men for the ministry, the best kind of men, more men and much better men, men of learning and character, able to teach with persuasive authority. It is not the voice of atheism we hear ; it is the voice of the Church that we miss. But, as Bishop Gore claims, most of the theological colleges are in the hands of the traditionalists, and the tendency of these colleges is to turn out priests rather than teachers, formalists rather than evangelists. Such colleges as represent the evangelical movement are, thanks to their title deeds, largely in the hands of pious laymen not very well educated, who adhere rigidly to a school of thought which is associated in the modern mind with an extreme of narrowness. Thus it comes about that many men who might serve the Church with great power are driven away at her doors. Something must be done to get men whose love of truth is a part of their love of God.

The second difficulty concerns the leadership of the Church. Bishops should be men with time to think, able when they address mankind to speak from " the top of the mind " ; scholars rather than administrators, saints rather than statesmen ; but such is the present condition that a man who is made a bishop finds himself so immersed in the business of a great institution that his intellectual and spiritual life become things of accident, luxurious things to be squeezed into the odd moments, if there are any, of an almost breathless day. This is not good for the Church. The world is not asking for mechanism. It is asking for light. It is, indeed, an over-organised world working in the dark.

Canon Barnes, however, is not concerned only with the theological aspects of Christianity. For him, religion is above all other things a social force, a great cleansing and sanctifying influence in the daily life of evolving man. One may obtain a just idea of his mind from a pronouncement he made at the last conference of Modern Churchmen :

> We cannot call ourselves Christians unless we recognise that we must preach the Gospel ; that we must go out and labour to bring men and women to Christ.
>
> The Kingdom of God is a social ideal.
>
> Modern Churchmen cannot stand aloof from intellectual, political, and economic problems.
>
> To bring the Gospel into the common life, to carry the message and sympathies of Jesus into the factory, the street, the house, is an urgent necessity in our age.

He sees Christianity, not as an interesting school of philosophy, not as a charming subject for brilliant and amicable discussions, but as a force essential to the salvation of mankind ; a force, however, which must first be disentangled from the accretions of ancient error before it can work its transforming miracles both in the heart of men and in the institutions of a materialistic civilisation. It is in order that it should thus work in the world, saving the world and fulfilling the purposes of God, that he labours in no particular school of the Church, to make the reasonableness of Christ a living possession of the modern mind.

Supreme in his character is that virtue Dr. Johnson observed and praised in a Duke of Devonshire —" a dogged veracity."

Chapter VIII

GENERAL BRAMWELL BOOTH

. . . for the generality of men, the attempt to live such a life would be a fatal mistake ; it would narrow instead of widening their minds, it would harden instead of soften-ing their hearts. Indeed, the effort " thus to go beyond themselves, and wind themselves too high," might even be followed by reaction to a life more profane and self-indulgent than that of the world in general.—Edward Caird.

Because General Booth wears a uniform he com-mands the public curiosity ; but because of that curiosity the public perhaps misses his considerable abilities and his singular attraction. His worst enemy is his frogged coat. Attention is diverted from his head to his epaulettes. He deserves, I am convinced, a more intelligent inquisitiveness.

To begin with, he is to be regarded as the original founder of that remarkable and truly catholic body of Christians known as the Salvation Army. His picturesque father and his wonderful mother were the humanity of that movement, but their son was its first impulse of spiritual fanaticism. The father was the dramatic " showman " of this movement, the son its fire. The mother endowed it with the energy of a deep and tender emotion, the son provided it with machinery.

It was Mr. Bramwell Booth, with his young friend Mr. Railton abetting him, who, discontented with the dullness and conservatism of the Christian Mission, drove the Reverend William Booth, an ex-Methodist minister preaching repentance in the slums, to fling restraint of every kind to the winds and to go in for religion as if it were indeed the only thing in the world that counted. William Booth at that time was forty-nine years of age.

Again, it was Mr. Bramwell Booth, working behind the scenes and pulling all the strings, who edged his father away from concluding an alliance with the Church of England in the early eighties. Archbishop Benson was anxious to conclude that alliance, on terms. The terms did not seem altogether onerous to the old General, who was rather fond of meeting dignitaries. But Mr. Bramwell Booth would hear of no concession which weakened the Army's authority in the slums, and which would also eventually weaken its authority in the world. He refused to acknowledge any service or rite of the Church as *essential* to the salvation of men. If the Lord's Supper were essential the Army would have it ; but the Army had proved that no other power was necessary to the working of miracles in the souls of men beyond the direct mercy of God acting on the centre of true penitence. He was the uncompromising protagonist of conversion, and his father came to agree with him.

Neither the old General nor his inspired wife,

admirable as revivalists, had the true fire of fanaticism in their blood.   They were too warm-hearted.
That strange unearthly fire burns only to its whitest
heat, perhaps, in veins which are cold and minds
which are hard.   It does not easily make its home
in benevolent and philanthropic natures, certainly
never in purely sentimental natures.   I think its
opening is made not by love but by hatred.   A man
may love God with all his heart, all his mind, and
all his soul, without feeling the spur of fanaticism
in his blood.   But let him hate sin with only a part
of his heart, mind, and soul, and he becomes a
fanatic.   His hatred will grow till it consumes his
whole being.

One need not be long in the company of General
Bramwell Booth to discover that he has two distinct
and separate manners, and that neither expresses
the whole truth of his rational life.   At one moment
he is full of cheerful good sense, the very incarnation
of jocular heartiness, a bluff, laughing, rallying,
chafing, and tolerant good fellow, overflowing with
the milk of human kindness, oozing with the honey
of social sweetness.   At the next moment, however,
the voice sinks suddenly to the key of what Father
Knox, I am afraid, would call unctimoniousness,
the eyelids flutter like the wings of a butterfly, the
whole plump pendulous face appears to vibrate
with emotion, the body becomes stiff with feeling,
the lips depressed with tragedy, and the dark eyes
shine with the suppressed tears of an unimaginable
pathos.

In both of these moments there is no pretence.
The two manners represent two genuine aspects

of his soul in its commerce with mankind. He believes that the world likes to be clapped on the shoulder, to be rallied on its manifest inconsistencies, and to have its hand wrung with a real heartiness. Also he believes that the heart of the world is sentimental, and that an authentic appeal in that quarter may lead to friendship—a friendship which, in its turn, may lead to business. Business is the true end of all his heartiness.

It is in his business manner that one gets nearer to the innermost secret of his nature. He is before everything else a superb man of business, far-seeing, practical, hard-headed, an organiser of victory, a statesman of the human soul. You cannot speak to him in this practical sphere without feeling that he is a man of the most unusual ability.

He can outline a complicated scheme with a precision and an economy of words which, he makes you feel, is a tribute to your perspicacity rather than a demonstration of his own powers of exposition. He comes quicker to the point than nine men of business out of ten. And he sticks to the main point with a tenacity which might be envied by every industrial magnate in the country.

Moreover, when it comes to your turn to speak he listens with the whole of his attention strung up to its highest pitch, his eyes wide open staring at you, his mouth pursed up into a little O of suction, his fingers pressing to his ear the receiver of a machine which overcomes his deafness, his whole body leaning half across the table in his eagerness to hear every word you say.

No sentiment shows in his face, no emotion sounds

in his voice. He is pure mind, a practical mind taut with attention. If he have occasion in these moments to ring the bell for an adjutant or a colonel, that official is addressed with the brevity and directness of a manager giving an order to his typist. Instead of a text over his mantelpiece one might expect to find the commercial legend, " Business Is Business."

Here, as I have said, one is nearer to the truth of his nature, for General Booth is an organiser who loves organisation, a diplomatist who delights in measuring his intelligence against the recalcitrance of mankind, a general who finds a deep satisfaction of soul in moving masses of men to achieve the purpose of his own design.

But even here one is not at the innermost secret of this extraordinary man's nature.

At the back of everything, I am convinced, is the cold and commanding intensity of a really great fanatic. He believes as no little child believes in God and Satan, Heaven and Hell, and the eternal conflict of God and Evil. He believes, too, as few priests of orthodox churches believe, that a man must in very truth be born again before he can inherit the Kingdom of Heaven ; that is to say, before he can escape the unimaginable agonies of an eternal dismissal from the Presence of God. But more than anything else he believes that sin is hateful ; a monstrous perversion to be attacked with all the fury of a good man's soul.

There is violence in his mind and violence in his religion. He believes in fighting the devil, and he delights in fighting him. I will not say that there is more joy at Salvation Army Headquarters over one poor miserable brand plucked from the burning than over ninety and nine cheques from wealthy subscribers ; but I am perfectly confident that the pleasure experienced at the sight of all those welcome cheques has its rise in the knowledge that money is power—power to fight the devil.

No man of my knowledge is so strangely blended as this genius of Salvation Army organisation. For although he is first and foremost a calm statesman of religious fervour, cool-headed, clear-eyed, and deliberative, a man profoundly inspired by hatred of evil, yet there are moments in his life of almost superhuman energy when the whole structure of his mind seems to give way, and the spirit appears like a child lost in a dark wood and almost paralysed with fear. Not seldom he was in his father's arms sobbing over the sufferings of humanity and the hardness of the world's heart, mingling his tears with his father's. Often in these late days he is in sore need of Mrs. Bramwell Booth's level-headed good sense to restore his exhausted emotions. And occasionally, like Lord Northcliffe, it is wise for him to get away from the Machine altogether, to travel far across the world or to rest in a cottage by the sea, waiting for a return of the energy which consumes him and yet keeps him alive.

It is possible to think that this formidable apostle of conversion is himself a divided self. His house of clay, one might almost suggest, is occupied by two tenants, one of whom would weep over sinners, while the other can serve God only by cudgelling the Devil back to hell with imprecations of a rich and florid nature. This stronger self, because of its cudgel, is in command of the situation, but the whimpering of the other is not to be stilled by blows which, however hearty and devastating, have not yet brought the devil to his knees.

It is interesting to sit in conversation with this devoted disciple of evangelicalism, and occasionally to lift one's eyes from his face to the portrait of his mother which hangs above his head. The two faces are almost identical, hauntingly identical ; so much so that one comes to regard the coachman-like whiskers clapped to the General's cheeks as in the nature of a disguise, thinking of him as his mother's eldest daughter rather than as his father's eldest son. There is certainly nothing about him which suggests the old General, and his mind is much more the mind of his mother—one of the most remarkable women in the world's history—than the mind of his father.

Catherine Booth was a zealot and at the heart of her theology a hard zealot. She believed that the physical agony of disease was a part of God's discipline, and that humanity is called upon to bear that fierce fire for the purification of its wicked spirit. She never flinched in confronting the theology of Methodism. She was in practice the tenderest of women, the most compassionate of missionaries, the most persuasive orator of the emotions in her day ; but in theory she was as hard as steel.

Her husband, on the other hand, who threw Jehovah's thunderbolts across the world as if he liked them, and approved of them, and was ready for any further number of these celestial missiles, of an even vaster displacement, was in his heart of hearts a wistful believer in everlasting mercy. Few men have been born with a softer heart. He sometimes wondered whether in framing the Regulations of the Salvation Army he had not pressed too hard on human nature. To the horrified scandal of his son, he even came to question, if only for a passing moment, the ordinance which forbids tobacco to the Salvationist.

He used to say in his old age, ruminating over the past, " Our standard is high. Our demand is hard ; aye, very hard. Yes, we don't mince matters in soul-saving. We demand the whole of a man, not a little bit of him, or three-fourths of him, or two-thirds of him ; we demand every drop of his blood and every beat of his heart and every thought of his brain. Yes, it's a hard discipline—hard because the standard is so high. I hope it is not too hard."

His son has never once, so far as my knowledge goes, questioned even the extremest of Salvation Army Regulations. The more extreme they are, the more they please him. It is one of his many good sayings that you cannot make a man clean by washing his shirt. His scrubbing brush is apt, I think, to remove some of the skin with the dirt. He believes without question that the only human test of conversion is the uttermost willingness of the soul to be spent in the service of soul-saving. If a man wishes to keep anything back from God, his heart is not given to God. He is no emotionalist in this matter. He uses emotion to break down the resistance of a sinner, but when once the surrender is made reason takes command of the illumined soul. He was asked on one occasion if he did not regard emotion as a dangerous thing. " Not when it is organised," was his reply.

The only concession he seems willing to make to the critics of the Salvation Army is in the matter of its hymns. He confesses that some of those hymns are crude and unlovely ; but examine this confession and you find that it is only the language which causes him uneasiness. Approach him on the subject of dogma, the dogma crudely expressed but truthfully expressed in the worst of those hymns, and he is as hard as Bishop Gore or Father Knox.

He has been too busy, I think, to hear even a whisper from the field of modernism, though exaggerated rumours of what is taking place in that field must occasionally reach his ear and confirm him in his obscurantism.

Perhaps it is all to the good that he should be thus wholly uninterested in the speculations of the trained theologian. He has other work to do, and work of great importance, with few rivals and no helpers. By the machine which he controls so admirably, men and women all over the world, and usually in the darkest places of the world, are turned from living disastrous lives, lives which too often involve the suffering of children, and encouraged and braced up to lead lives of great beauty and an extreme of self-sacrifice.

He does well, I think, to stick with the unwavering and uncompromising tenacity of a fanatic to that centre of the Christian religion from which was derived in the first two centuries of its great history almost all impetus which enabled it to escape from Judaism and conquer the world. It is still true, and I suppose it will remain true to the end of time, that man born of a woman must be born again of the spirit if he is to pass from darkness into light. This, after all, is the whole thesis of Salvationism, and if General Booth wavered here the Army would be scattered to the winds. As for his definitions of light and darkness, at this stage of the world's journey we need not be too nice in our acceptance of them.

But there remains the important question of Salvation Army methods.

It seems to me that here a change is desirable, not a radical change, for many of those methods are admirable enough, particularly those of which the public too seldom hears, but a change all the same, and one deep enough to create fresh sympathy for this devoted movement of evangelical Christianity.

I think it is time to stop praying and preaching at street corners, to mitigate the more brazen sounds of the Army band, and to discountenance all colloquialisms in Salvationist propaganda. I do not wish, God forbid, to make the Army respectable ; I wish it to remain exactly where it is—but with a greater quietness and a deeper, more personal sympathy in its appeal to the sad and the sorrowful.

General Booth is not the man to make these changes, but his wife is a woman who might. In any case they will be made. Time will bring them about. Then it will be seen, I think, that the Salvation Army is one of the most powerful agencies in the world for spreading the good news of personal religion among the depressed millions of the human race. For even at this present time the lasting work of the Salvationist, the work which makes him so noble and so useful a figure in the modern world, is not accomplished by pageantry and tub-thumping, but by the intimate, often most beautiful, and very little known work of its slum officers, particularly the women.

Finally, concerning the General, he is in himself a telling witness to one of the mysterious powers of the Christian religion. For he is surely by temperament one of the most unstable of minds, and yet by the power of religion he has become a coherent personality of almost rigid singleness of purpose. In conversation with him one cannot help feeling that he is jumpy and excitable ; every movement of his extremely mobile face suggests a soul of gutta-percha stretched in all directions by the movements of his brain, and twitching with every thought that crosses his mind ; but at the same time one is aware in him of a power which is never deflected by a hair's breadth from the path of a single purpose, and which holds him together with a strength that may be weakened but that can never be broken.

His supreme value for the student of religion is to be found in the explanation of this unifying power. In spite of intellectual shortcomings which might seem almost to exclude him from the serious attention of educated people, he stands out with a marked emphasis from the company of far abler men by reason of this power—this sense of unusual vigour and abnormal concentration of strength. And the explanation of this power, which unifies an otherwise incoherent personality, is to be found, I am quite confident, in his burning hatred of iniquity.

As a boy, like the poet Gray and the late Lord Salisbury, he suffered a good deal of bullying, and thus learned at school something beyond the reach of the Latin Grammar, namely, the brutality of human nature. He has never forgotten that discovery. Indeed, his after-life has widened and intensified that early lesson. Sin is brutality. It is selfishness seeking its low pleasure and its base delight in vilest self-indulgence involving the suffering of others, sometimes their profoundest degradation, even their absolute destruction. Particularly did he experience this burning conviction when he came to understand the well-nigh inconceivable brutality of sexual vice. I believe that it was a poor harlot in the slums of London who first opened for him the door of fanaticism.

He had longed as a schoolboy to hit back at his tyrants, and now in the dawn of manhood that long repression made its weight felt in the blows he showered on the face of evil. For a year or two he was a wild man of evangelicalism, leading attacks on evil, challenging public attention, seeking imprisonment, courting martyrdom. It was from the flaming indignation of his soul that Mr. Stead took fire, and led a crusade against impurity which shocked the conscience of the eighties. But so

deep and eternal was this hatred of evil, that
General Booth soon came to see that he must
express it in some manner which would outlive the
heady moments of a " lightning campaign." He
settled down to express that profound abhorrence
of iniquity in terms of organisation. Tares might
be torn suddenly from the human heart, but not
the root of evil. If he could not kill the devil, at
least he could circumvent him.

Such intense hatred of evil as still consumes his
being is not popular in these days, and may perhaps
be regarded as irrational. But we should do well
to remind ourselves that while those who regard
evil merely as a vestigial memory of human evolution do little or nothing to check its ravages, men
like General Booth, and the men and women
inspired by his abhorrence, save every year from
physical and moral destruction thousands of
unhappy people who become at once the apostles
of an extreme goodness.

Such evidences of mediocrity as exist in the
Salvationist are purely intellectual ; morally and
spiritually he is in the advance guard of the human
race.

Chapter IX

DR. W. E. ORCHARD

O, you poor creatures in the large cities of wide-world politics, you young, gifted, ambition-tormented men, who consider it your duty to give your opinion on everything that occurs ; who, by thus raising dust and noise, mistake yourselves for the chariot of history ; who, being always on the look-out for an opportunity to put in a word or two, lose all true productiveness. However desirous you may be of doing great deeds, the profound silence of pregnancy never comes to you. The event of the day sweeps you along like chaff, while you fancy that you are chasing it.— NIETZSCHE.

UNTIL quite the other day I looked upon Dr. Orchard as a person unique in his generation. But I am now told by an authority in the non-conformist world that there are " two others of him "—one, I think, in Birmingham, the second in Clapham.

I am still permitted to think, however, that to Dr. Orchard belongs the distinction of being the first person of this erratic trinity, and therefore we may still regard him with that measure of curiosity which is the tribute paid by simple people to the eccentric and the abnormal.

But let me warn the reader against expectations

of an original genius.   Dr. Orchard does not create ;
he copies.   His innovations are all made after visits
to the lumber-room.   It is by going back such a
long distance into the past that he startles, and
by coming round full circle that he appears to
surprise the future.

But where originality is rare, eccentricity must
not be discounted.

Dr. Orchard is a ritualist in the midst of nonconformity ; the first Free Churchman, I believe,
to entertain exalted ceremonial aspirations, and
to kneel for his orders at the feet of an orthodox
bishop.   One might almost hazard the conjecture
that he remains in the Congregationalist Communion,
as so many Anglo-Catholics remain in the Establishment, solely to supply the fermentation of an idea
which will shatter its present constitution.   One
thinks of him as a repentant Cromwell restoring
" that bauble " to its accustomed place on the
table of tradition.

In his heart of hearts he would appear to be a
fervent institutionalist, a lover of ceremonial, and
a convinced sacerdotalist.   To hear him use the
word Catholic is to make one understand how the
Church of Rome dazzles certain eyes, and to hear
him claim that he is in the apostolical succession
is to make one realise afresh how broad is the way
of credulity.

One may understand his dislike of the hideous
and pretentious architecture which disgraces nonconformity, and sympathise with his desire for
more beautiful services in nonconformist chapels ;
but it is not so easy, while he remains a

nonconformist, to understand, or to feel any considerable degree of sympathy with, his tendency towards
practices which are the very antithesis of the
nonconformist tradition.

All the same he is a person of whom we should
do well to take at least a passing notice, for he
witnesses, however extravagantly, to a movement
in the Free Churches which is not likely to lose
momentum with the next few years—a movement
not only away from sectarian isolation but towards
the idea of one catholic and apostolic Church.
There is certainly unrest in the Free Churches,
and Dr. Orchard is a straw which helps us to understand if not the permanent direction of the wind,
at least the fact that there is a breeze blowing in
the fields of religious freedom.

Not long ago I asked one of the greatest figures
in the Anglican Church what he thought of Dr.
Orchard. He replied by raising his eyebrows and
exclaiming rather disdainfully : " A ritualistic
Dissenter ! What is it possible to think of him ? "
I said that he attracted a good many people to his
services in the King's Weigh House Church, and that
I had heard Mrs. Asquith was sometimes a member
of his congregation. " *That*," answered the dig-
nitary, " would not make me think any higher of
Dr. Orchard."

For many people, it must be confessed, he is a
slightly ludicrous figure. He presents the spectacle
of a sparrow stretching its wings and opening its beak
to imitate the eagle of catholic lecterns. And he has
a singularly nettling manner with some people which
must add, I should think, to this unpopularity He

seems sweepingly satisfied with himself and his opinions, which are mostly of a challenging nature. He does not discuss but attempts to browbeat. His voice is an argument, and the expression on his face and the fire in his eyes suggest the street corner. He would have greatly distressed a man like Matthew Arnold, for the only method against such didactics is to send for the boxing gloves.

All the same he is a man of no little force, perhaps a scattered and dispersed force, as I am inclined to think ; and he is a fighter whose blows, if not a teacher whose opinions, are more worthy of attention than his sacerdotal pretensions might lead one to suppose.

In appearance he may be compared with Dr. Clifford, but Dr. Clifford reduced to youthfulness and multiplied by an infinite cocksureness ; a small, eager, sandy-haired, clean-shaven, boyish-looking man, with light-coloured eyes behind shining spectacles, the head craning forward, the body elastic and restless with inexhaustible energy, the whole of him—body, mind, and spirit—tremulous with a jerkiness of being which seems to have no effect whatever on his powers of endurance.

One misses in him all feeling, all tone, of mellowness. His mind, at present, shows no lightest trace of the hallowing marks of time ; it suggests rather the very architecture he takes so savage a pleasure in denouncing—a kind of mock Gothic mind, an Early Doulton personality. He has a thin voice, rather husky, and a recent accent.

In his most vigorous moments, when he is bubbling over with epigrams and paradoxes, ridiculing the

dull people who do not agree with him, and laughing
to scorn those who think they can maintain the
Christian spirit outside the mysterious traditions
of the Catholic Church, or when he is describing a
recent church as a Blancmange Cathedral, and
paraphrasing an account, given I think by Mr.
James Douglas, of the building of a certain tabernacle
in London—first it started out to be a Jam
Factory, then a happy idea occurred to the builder
that he should turn it into a Waterworks, then the
foreman suggested that it would make an ideal
swimming-bath, but finally the architect came on
the scene and said, " Here, half a minute ; there's
an alteration wanted here ; we're going to make it
into a church "—at such moments, Dr. Orchard
might be likened to a duodecimo Chesterton—but
a Chesterton of nonconformity. For he is a little
crude, a little recent ; a mind without mellowness,
a spirit without beauty, a soul which feeds upon
aggression.

He makes an amusing figure with a black cloak
wrapped round his little body in Byronic folds,
and a soft hat of black plush on his head, a Vesta
Tilley quickness informing both his movements and
his speech, as he nips forward in conversation with
a friend, the arms, invisible beneath their cloak,
pressed down in front of him, his body leaning
forward, his peering eyes dancing behind their
spectacles.

Nevertheless, those who most find him only
amusing or worse still thoroughly dislikeable, who
are antipathetic to the whole man, and who thus cannot come at the secret of his influence, must confess

that there is nothing about him either of the smooth and oily or of the adroit and compromising. He is the last man on earth to be called an opportunist. This is in his favour. His aggressiveness must put all but the toughest against him. He is tremendously in earnest. It would be difficult I think to exceed his sincerity.

But not to mind whose toes one may tread on is hardly in the style of St. Francis ; and, after all, it is possible to be tremendously earnest about wrong things, and consumingly sincere in matters which are not perhaps definitely certain to advance the higher life of the human race. Humility is always safest ; indeed, it is essential to all earnestness and sincerity, if those energies are not to repel as many as they attract.

Dr. Orchard's manner, which can be extraordinarily nettling in conversation, as I have suggested, is evidently of a very soothing character in the confessional—if that is the proper term. He has a remarkable following among women, and it is said that " if he put a brass plate on his door and charged five guineas a time " he might be one of the richest mind-doctors in London. He himself declares that his real work is almost entirely personal. I have heard him speak with some contempt of preaching, quoting the witticism of a friend that " Anglican preaching is much worse than it really need be," or words to that effect. He likes ceremonial and private confidence. He has the instincts of a priest.

His patients appear to be the wreckage of psychoanalysis. It is said that " half the neurotics of

London " consult him about their souls. I have
no idea of the manner in which he treats these unhappy people, but I am perfectly sure that he gives
them counsel of a healthy nature. There is nothing
about him which suggests unwholesomeness,
and much that suggests sound strength and clean
good sense. Also among his penitents are numerous
shopgirls who have lost in the commercial struggle
whatever piety they possessed in childhood and in
their craving for excitement have gone astray from
the path of safe simplicity—gambling on horse races
and often getting into serious trouble by their losses.
Dr. Orchard may be trusted to give these weak,
rather than erring daughters of London, advice which
would commend itself to the Free Church Council,
for with all his sacerdotal aberrations the basis of
his moral life is rooted in Puritanism.

It is an entirely good thing that there should be a
minister of religion in London who attracts people
of this order, particularly a minister whose moral
notions are so eminently sane and so steadily uncompromising. London is stronger and less disreputable
for Dr. Orchard's presence in its midst—no doubt a
very vulgar, degrading, and trivial midst, but all
the same a great congestion of little people, one
where the solemn note of the old morality sounds
all too seldom across the tinkle of bells in the caps
of so many fools.

This moral influence, however, may appear questionable in the eyes of strong-minded and unsenti-
mental people. Would he exercise such personal
power, it may be asked, if he were not regarded as
a " novelty," if the eccentricity of his position in

the nonconformist world had not so skilfully adver-
tised him to a light and foolish generation ever
ready to run after what is new ? Of an Anglican
clergyman's popularity I have heard it said, " Who
could not fill a church with the help of the band of
the Grenadier Guards ? "

I should not like to answer this question, and yet
I do not like to pass it by. Antipathetic as I find
myself to Dr. Orchard, it would not be just to imply
that the power of his personal influence is not a
great one, and one of an entirely wholesome nature.
It seems to me, then, that the nature of that which
attracts the unhappy to seek his counsel is of small
moment in comparison with the extent and beneficence of his good counsel. The fact that he does
help people, does save many people from very
unhappy and dangerous situations, is a fact which
gives him a title not only to our respect, but to our
gratitude.

Perhaps it is his knowledge of all this petty misery
and sordid unwholesomeness which makes him disposed at times, in spite of an almost rollicking temperament, to take dismal and despairing views of
the religious future.

I have heard him say with some bitterness that
people do not know what Christianity is, that it
has been so misrepresented to them, and so mixed
up with the quarrels of sectarianism, that the heart
of it is really non-existent for the multitude. He
speaks with impatience of the nonconformist
churches and with contempt of the Anglican church.
We are all wrong together. Organised religion, he
feels, is hanging over the abyss of destruction,

while the nation looks on with an indifference which should complete its self-contempt.

His quarrel, however, is not only with the churches, but with the nation as well. He regards the system under which we live as thoroughly unchristian. It is the system of mammon—a system of frank, brutal, and insolent materialism. Why do we put up with it ?

His religious sense is so outraged by this system of economic individualism that he bursts out with irritable impatience against those who speak of infusing into it a more Christian spirit. For him the whole body of our industrialism is rotten with selfishness and covetousness, the high note of service entirely absent from it, the one energy which informs it the energy of aggressive self-seeking. Such a system cannot be patched. It is anti-Christian. It should be smashed.

He plunges into economics with a good deal of vigour, but I do not think he has thought out to its logical conclusion his thesis of guild socialism. Perhaps his tone is here more vehement than his knowledge of a notoriously difficult science altogether justifies.

He opposes himself to the evolutionary philosophy of the nineteenth century, and is ready to defend the idea of a Fall of Man. His contribution to theology is a quibble. The old dogmas are to stand : only the language is to be adjusted to the modern intelligence. You may picture him with drawn sword—a sword tempered in inquisitorial fires— standing guard over his quibble and ready to defend it with his spiritual life.

His opinions are apt to place him among minorities. He was against the War, and during that
long-drawn agony attracted to himself the mild
attention of the authorities. I believe he likened
the great struggle to a battle between Sodom and
Gomorrah. However, he was careful not to go so
far as Mr. Bertrand Russell. As he himself says,
" I don't mind dying for Jesus Christ, but not for
making a silly ass of myself."

He occasionally writes reviews for *The Nation*,
and has published a number of uneventful books.
His writing is not distinguished or illuminating.
With a pen in his hand he loses all his natural force.
He writes, I think, as one who feels that he is wasting
time. Like Mr. Winston Churchill, he diverts his
leisure with a paintbrush.

One is disposed to judge that the mind of this very
fiery particle is too busy with side-issues to make
acquaintance with the deeper mysteries of his
religion. When he complains that people do not
know what Christianity is, one wonders whether
his own definition would satisfy the saints. He is a
fighter rather than a teacher, a man of action rather
than a seer. I do not think he could be happy in a
world which presented him with no opportunities
for punching heads.

Matthew Arnold, quoting from *The Times* a
sentence to the effect that the chief Dissenting
ministers are becoming quite the intellectual equals
of the ablest of the clergy, referred it to the famous
Dr. Dale of Birmingham, and remarked : " I have no
fears concerning Mr. Dale's intellectual muscles ;
what I am a little uneasy about is his religious

temper. The essence of religion is grace and peace."

But Dr. Orchard, we must not fail to see, is quite genuinely exasperated by the deadness of religious life, and is straining every nerve to quicken the soul of Christ's sleeping Church. This discontent of his is an important symptom, even if his prescription, a very old one, gives no hope of a cure. He is popular, influential, a figure of the day, and still young ; yet his soul is full of rebellion and his heart is swelling with the passion of mutiny. Something is evidently not right. Quite certainly he has not discovered the peace that passes understanding.

But perhaps Dr. Orchard will never be satisfied till all men think as he thinks, and until there is only one Church in the world for the expression of spiritual life, with either Bishop Herford or himself for its pope.

In the meantime he is too busy for the profound silence. The event of the day sweeps him before it.

CHAPTER X

BISHOP TEMPLE

. . . faint, pale, embarrassed, exquisite Pater! He reminds me, in the disturbed midnight of our actual literature, of one of those lucent match-boxes which you place, on going to bed, near the candle, to show you, in the darkness, where you can strike a light: he shines in the uneasy gloom—vaguely, and has a phosphorescence, not a flame. But I quite agree with you that he is not of the little day—but of the longer time.—HENRY JAMES.

THE future of Bishop Temple is of more importance to the Church than to himself. He is one of those solid and outstanding men whose decisions affect a multitude, a man to whom many look with a confidence which he himself, perhaps, may never experience.

He cannot, I think, be wholly unaware of this consideration in forming his judgments, and I attribute, rather to a keen and weighty sense of great responsibility than to any lack of vital courage, his increasing tendency towards the Catholic position. One begins to think that he is likely to disappoint many of those who once regarded him as the future statesman of a Christianity somewhat less embarrassed by institutionalism.

It is probable, one fears, that he may conclude at Lambeth a career in theology comparable with that of Mr. Winston Churchill in politics. Born in the ecclesiastical purple he may return to it, bringing with him only the sheaves of an already mouldering orthodoxy.

On one ground, however, there is hope that he may yet shine in our uneasy gloom with something more effective than the glow of phosphorescence. He is devoted heart and soul to Labour. Events, then, may drive him out of his present course, and urge him towards a future of signal usefulness; for Labour is a force which waits upon contingency, and moves as the wind moves—now softly, then harshly, now gently, then with great violence. Those who go with Labour are not like travellers in the Tory coach or the Liberal tram; they are like passengers in a balloon.

I do not mean that Bishop Temple will ever be so far swept out of his course as to find himself among the revolutionaries; he carries too much weight for that, is, indeed, too solid a man altogether for any lunatic flights to the moon; I mean, rather, that where the more reasonable leaders of Labour are compelled to go by the force of political and industrial events, William Temple is likely to find that he himself is also expected, nay, but obliged to go, and very easily that may be a situation from which the Lollard Tower of Lambeth Palace will appear rather romantically if not altogether hopelessly remote.

His career, then, like Mr. Winston Churchill's in politics, is still an open event, and therefore a matter for interesting speculation. This fair-haired, fresh-faced, and boylike Bishop of Manchester, smiling at us behind his spectacles, the square head very upright, the broad shoulders well back, the whole short stocky figure like a rock, confronts us with something of the challenge of the Sphinx.

One of the chief modernists said to me the other day : " Temple is the most dangerous man in the Church of England. He is not only a socialist, he is also Gore's captive, bow and spear." But another, by no means an Anglo-Catholic, corrected this judgment. " Temple," said he, " is not yet hopelessly Catholic. He has, indeed, attracted to himself by his Christlike attitude towards Non-conformists the inconvenient attentions of that remarkable person the Bishop of Zanzibar. His sympathies with Labour, which are the core of his being, are sufficient reason for ——'s mistrust of him. I do not at all regard him as dangerous. On the contrary, I think he is one of the most interesting men in the Church, and also, which is far more important, one of its most promising leaders."

So many men, so many opinions. Strangely enough it is from an Anglo-Catholic who is also a Labour enthusiast that I hear the fiercest and most uncompromising criticism of this young Bishop of Manchester.

" All his successes have been failures. He went to Repton with a tremendous reputation ; did nothing ; went to St. James's, Piccadilly, as a man who would set the Thames on fire, failed, and went to Westminster with a heightened reputation ; left it for the Life and Liberty Movement, which has done nothing, and then on to Manchester as the future Archbishop of Canterbury. What has he done ? What has he ever done ?

" He can't stick at anything ; certainly he can't stick at his job—always he must be doing something else. I don't regard him as a reformer. I regard him as a talker. He has no strength. Sometimes I think he has no heart. Intellectual, yes ; but intellectual without pluck. I don't know how his brain works. I give that up. I agree, he joined the Labour movement before he was ordained. There I think he is sincere, perhaps devoted. But is there any heart in his devotion ? Do the poor love him ? Do the Labour leaders hail him as a leader ? I don't think so. Perhaps I'm prejudiced. Whenever I go to see him, he gives me the impression that he has got his watch in his hand or his eye on the clock. An inhuman sort of person— no warmth, no sympathy, not one tiniest touch of tenderness in his whole nature. No. Willie Temple is the very man the Church of England *doesn't* want."

Finally, one of those men in the Anglo-Catholic Party to whom Dr. Temple looks up with reverence and devotion, said to me in the midst of generous laudation : " His trouble is that he doesn't concentrate. He is inclined to leave the main thing. But I hear he is really concentrating on his work at Manchester, and therefore I have hopes that he will justify the confidence of his friends. He is certainly a very able man, very ; there can be no question of that."

It will be best, I think, to glance first of all at this question of ability.

Dr. Temple has a notable gift of rapid statement and pellucid exposition. One doubts if many theologians in the whole course of Christian history have covered more ground more trippingly than Dr. Temple covers in two little books called *The Faith and Modern Thought*, and *The Kingdom of God*. His wonderful powers of succinct statement may perhaps give the impression of shallowness ; but this is an entirely false impression—no impression could indeed be wider of the mark. His learning, though not so wide as Dean Inge's, nor so specialised as the learning of Canon Barnes, is nevertheless true learning, and learning which has been close woven into the fabric of his intellectual life. There are but few men in the Church of England who have a stronger grip on knowledge ; and very few, if any at all, who can more clearly and vividly express in simple language the profoundest truths of religion and philosophy.

In order to show his quality I will endeavour to summarise his arguments for the Existence of God, with as many quotations from his writings as my space will permit.

" It is not enough to prove," he says, " that some sort of Being exists. In the end, the only thing that matters is the character of that Being." But how are we to set out on this quest since " Science will not allow us a starting point at all " ?

He answers that question by carrying the war into the scientific camp, as he has a perfect right to do. " Science makes one colossal assumption always ; science assumes that the world is rational in this sense, that when you have thought out thoroughly the implications of your experience, the result is fact. . . . That is the basis of all science ; it is a colossal assumption, but science cannot move one step without it."

Science begins with its demand that the world should be seen as coherent ; it insists on looking at it, on investigating it, till it is so seen. As long as there is any phenomenon left out of the systematic coherence that you have discovered, science is discontented and insists that either the system is wrongly or imperfectly conceived or else the facts have not been correctly stated.

This demand for " a coherent and comprehensive statement of the whole field of fact " comes solely from reason. How do we get it ? We have no ground in experience for insisting that the world shall be regarded as intelligent, as " all hanging together and making up one system." But reason insists upon it. This gives us " a kinship between the mind of man and the universe he lives in."

Now, when man puts his great question to the universe, and to every phenomenon in that universe, *Why ?*—Why is this what it is, what my reason recognises it to be ? is he not in truth asking, What is this thing's purpose ? What is it doing in the universe ? What is its part in the coherent system of all-things-together ?

Now there is in our experience already one principle which does answer the question " Why ? " in such a way as to raise no further questions ; that is, the principle of Purpose. Let us take a very simple illustration. Across many of the hills in Cumberland the way from one village to another is marked by white stones placed at short intervals. We may easily imagine a simple-minded person asking how they came there, or what natural law could account for their lying in that position ; and the physical antecedents of the fact—the geological history of the stones and the physiological structure of the men who moved them—give no answer. As soon, however, as we hear that men placed them so, to guide way-farers in the mist or in the night, our minds are satisfied.

Dr. Temple holds fast to that great word, that infallible clue, Purpose. He is not arguing from design. He keeps his feet firmly on scientific ground, and asks, as a man of science asks, What is this ? and Why is this ? Then he finds that this question can proceed only from faith in coherence, and discovers that the quest of science is quest of Purpose.

To investigate Purpose is obviously to acknowledge Will.

Science requires, therefore, that there should be a real Purpose in the world. . . . It appears from the investigation of science, from investigation of the method of scientific procedure itself, that there must be a Will in which the whole world is rooted and grounded ; and that we and all other things proceed therefrom ; because only so is there even a hope of attaining the intellectual satisfaction for which science is a quest.

Reason is obliged to confess the hypothesis of a Creative Will, although it does not admit that man has in any way perceived it. But is this hypothesis, which is essential to science, to be left in the position of Mahomet's coffin ? Is it not to be investigated ? For if atheism is irrational, agnosticism is not scientific—" it is precisely a refusal to apply the scientific method itself beyond a certain point, and that a point at which there is no reason in heaven or earth to stop."

To speak about an immanent purpose is very good sense ; but to speak about a purpose behind which there is no Will is nonsense.

People, he says, become so much occupied with the consideration of what they know that they entirely forget " the perfectly astounding fact that they know it." Also they overlook or slur the tremendous fact of spiritual individuality ; " because I am I, I am not anybody else." But let the individual address to himself the question he puts to the universe, let him investigate his own pressing sense of spiritual individuality, just as he investigates any other natural phenomenon, and he will find himself applying that principle of Purpose, and thinking of himself in relation to the Creator's Will.

If there is Purpose in the universe there is Will ; you cannot have Purpose or intelligent direction, without Will. But, as we have seen, " to speak about an immanent will is nonsense " :

It is the purpose, the meaning and thought of God, that is immanent not God Himself. He is not limited to the world that He has made ; He is beyond it, the source and ground of it all, but not it. Just as you may say that in Shakespeare's work his thoughts and feelings are immanent ; you find them there in the book, but you don't find Shakespeare, the living, thinking, acting man, in the book. You have to infer the kind of being that he was from what he wrote ; he himself is not there ; his thoughts are there.

He pronounces " the most real of all problems," the problem of evil, to be soluble. *Why is there no problem of good ?* Note well, that " the problem of evil is always a problem in terms of purpose." How evil came does not matter : the question is, Why is it here ? What is it doing ? " While we are sitting at our ease it generally seems to us that the world would be very much better if all evil were abolished. . . . But would it ? "

> Surely we know that one of the best of the good things in life is victory, and particularly moral victory. But to demand victory without an antagonist is to demand something with no meaning. . . .
>
> If you take all the evil out of the world you will remove the possibility of the best thing in life. That does not mean that evil is good. What one means by calling a thing good is that the spirit rests permanently content with it for its own sake. Evil is precisely that with which no spirit can rest content ; and yet it is the condition, not the accidental but the essential condition, of what is in and for itself the best thing in life, namely moral victory.

His definition of Sin helps us to understand his politics :

> Sin is the self-assertion either of a part of a man's nature against the whole, or of a single member of the human family against the welfare of that family and the will of its Father.

But if it is self-will, he asks, how is it to be overcome ?

> Not by any kind of force ; for force cannot bend the will. Not by any kind of external transaction ; that may remit the penalty, but will not of itself change the will. It must be by the revelation of a love so intense that no heart which beats can remain indifferent to it.

All this seems to me admirably said. It does at

least show that there are clear, logical, and practical reasons for the religious hypothesis. The mind of man, seeking to penetrate the physical mysteries of the universe, encounters Mind. Mind meets Mind. Reason recognises, if it does not always salute, Reason. And in this rational and evolving universe the will of man has a struggle with itself, a struggle on which man clearly sees the fortunes of his progress, both intellectual and spiritual, depend. Will recognises Will. And surveying the history of his race he comes to a standstill of love and admiration before only one life—

> a life whose historic occurrence is amply demonstrated, whose moral and spiritual pre-eminence consists in the completeness of self-sacrifice, and whose inspiration for those who try to imitate it is without parallel in human experience.

Love recognises Love. " I am the Light of the World."

I will give a few brief quotations from Dr. Temple's pages showing how he regards the revelation of the Creative Will made by Christ, Who " in His teaching and in His Life is the climax of human ethics."

> Love, and the capacity to grow in love, is the whole secret.
> The one thing demanded is always the power to grow. Growth and progress in the spiritual life is the one thing Christ is always demanding.
> He took bread and said that it was His body ; and He gave thanks for it, He broke it, and He gave it to them and said, " Do this in remembrance of Me." . . . Do what ? . . . The demand is nothing less than this, that men should take their whole human life, and break it, and give it for the good of others.

The growth in love, and the sacrifice which evokes that growth in love, are, I would suggest, the most precious things in life. Take away the condition of this and you will destroy the value of the spiritual world.

One may form, I think, a true judgment of the man from these few extracts.

He is one who could not move an inch without a thesis, and who moves only by inches even when he has got his thesis. His intellect, I mean, is in charge of him from first to last. He feels deeply, not sharply. He loves truly, not passionately. With his thesis clear in his mind, he draws his sword, salutes the universe, kneels at the cross, and then, with joy in his heart, or rather a deep and steady sense of well-being, moves forward to the world, prepared to fight. Fighting is the thing. Yes, but here is neither Don Quixote nor Falstaff. He will fight warily, take no unnecessary risk, and strike only when he is perfectly sure of striking home.

You must not think of him as old beyond his years (he is only a little over forty) but rather as one who was wise from his youth up. He has never flung himself with emotion into any movement of the human mind, not because he lacks devotion, but because he thinks the victories of emotion are often defeats in disguise. He wishes to be certain. He will fight as hard as any man, but intelligently, knowing that it will be a fight to the last day of his life. He is perhaps more careful to last than to win—an ecclesiastical Jellicoe rather than a Beatty. Nor, I think, must one take the view of the critic that he has never stuck to the main point. Every step in his career, as I see it, has been towards opportunity—the riskless opportunity of greater service and freer movement.

I regard him as a man whose full worth will never be known till he is overtaken by a crisis. I can see him moving smoothly and usefully in times of comparative peace to the Primacy, holding that high office with dignity, and leaving behind him a memory that will rapidly fade. But I cannot see him so clearly in the midst of a storm. A great industrial upheaval, for example, where would that land him ? The very fact that one does not ask, How would he direct it ? shows perhaps the measure of distrust one may feel in his strength—not of character—but of personality. He would remain, one is sure, a perfectly good man, and a man of intelligence ; but would any great body of the nation feel that it would follow him either in a fight or in a retreat ? I am not sure. On the whole I feel that his personality is not so effective as it might have been if he had not inherited the ecclesiastical tradition, had not been born in the episcopal purple.

By this I mean that he gives me the feeling of a man who is not great, but who has the seeds of greatness in him. Events may prove him greater than even his warmest admirers now imagine him to be. A crisis, either in the Church or in the economic world, might enable him to break through a certain atmosphere of traditional clericalism which now rather blurs the individual outline of his soul. But, even with the dissipation of this atmosphere, one is not quite sure that the outline of his soul would not follow the severe lines of a High Anglican tradition. He does not, at present, convince one of original force.

Yet, when all doubts are expressed, he remains one of the chief hopes of the Church, and so perhaps of the nation. For from his boyhood up the Kingdom of God has meant to him a condition here upon earth in which the soul of man, free from all oppression, can reach gladly up towards the heights of spiritual development.

He hates in his soul the miserable state to which a conscienceless industrialism has brought the daily life of mankind. He lays it down that " it is the duty of the Church to make an altogether new effort to realise and apply to all the relations of life its own positive ideal of brotherhood and fellowship." To this end he has brought about an important council of masters and men who are investigating with great thoroughness the whole economic problem, so thoroughly that the Bishop will not receive their report, I understand, till 1923—a report which may make history.

As a member of the Society of Spirits, he says, " I have a particular destiny to fulfil." He is a moral being, conscious of his dependence on other men. He traces the historic growth of the moral judgment :

> The growth of morality is twofold. It is partly a growth in content, from negative to positive. It is partly a growth in extent, from tribal to universal. And in both of these forms of growth it is accompanied, and as a rule, though my knowledge would not entitle me to say always, it is also conditioned by a parallel development in religious conviction.

We are all aware that early morality is mainly negative; it is the ruling out of certain ways of arriving at the human ideal, however that is to be defined, which have been attempted and have been found failures. Whatever else may be the way to reach the end, murder is not, theft is not, and so on. Thus we get the Second Table of the Decalogue, where morality commits itself to prohibitions—this is not the way, that is not the way; then gradually, under the pressure of experience, there begins to emerge the conception of the end which makes all this prohibition necessary, and which these methods when they were attempted failed to reach. . . .

And so we come at last to " the Kingdom of God as proclaimed by Christ, and the supreme law of ethics, the demonstrably final law of ethics, is laid down—Thou shalt love thy neighbour as thyself."

Of course the words come from the Old Testament. Some critics used to say : " You will find in the Rabbis almost everything, if not quite everything, which you find in the teaching of Christ." " Yes," added Wellhausen, " and how much else besides." It was the singling out of this great principle and laying the whole emphasis upon it that made the difference.

To a man who believes that Christ came to set up the Kingdom of God, clearly neither the Conservative nor Liberal Party can appeal with any compelling force of divinity. How far the Labour Party may appeal must depend, I should think, on the man's knowledge of economic law. As Dean Inge says, Christ's sole contribution to economics is " Beware of covetousness "—an injunction which the Labour Party has not yet quite taken to its heart. But Dr. Temple has a right to

challenge his clerical critics for Christ's sanction of
the present system, which is certainly founded on
covetousness and produces strikingly hideous results.

His theological position may be gathered from
the following reply which he made, as a Canon of
Westminster, to a representative of the *Daily
Telegraph* nearly two years ago. I do not think
he has greatly changed. He was asked how far
the Church could go in meeting that large body
of opinion which cannot accept some of its chief
dogmas. He replied :

> I can speak freely, because I happen to hold two
> of the dogmas which most people quarrel about—
> the virgin birth and the physical resurrection. There
> are other heresies floating about ! One of our deans
> is inclined to assert the finitude of God, and another
> to deny anything in the nature of personality to God
> or to man's spirit ! Rather confusing ! Philosophic
> questions of this kind, however, do not greatly concern
> mankind. To believe in God the Father is essential
> to the Christian religion. Other doctrines may not
> be so essential, but they must not be regarded as
> unimportant. Personally, I wish the Church to hold
> her dogmas, because I would do nothing to widen
> the gulf which separates us from the other great
> Churches, the Roman and the Eastern. The greatest
> political aim of humanity, in my opinion, is a super-
> state, and that can only come through a Church
> universal. How we all longed for it during the war !
> —one voice above the conflict, the voice of the
> Church, the voice of Christ ! If the Pope had only
> spoken out, with no reference to the feelings of the
> Austrian Emperor !—what a gain that would have
> been for religion. But the great authentic voice
> never sounded. Instead of the successor of St. Peter
> we had to content ourselves with the American Press
> —excellent, no doubt, but hardly satisfying.

Let me tell you a rather striking remark by an
Italian friend of mine, an editor of an Italian review,
and not a Roman Catholic. He was saying that every
Church that persisted for any time possessed something essential to the religion of Christ. I asked him
what he saw in the Roman Church that was essential.
He replied at once, ' The Papacy.' I was surprised for
the moment, but I saw presently what he meant. The
desire of the world is for universal peace, universal
harmony. Can that ever be achieved by a disunited
Christendom? The nations are rivals. Their rivalry
persisted at the Peace Conference, disappointing all
the hopes of idealists. Must it not always persist,
must not horrible carnage, awful desolation, ruinous
destruction, and, at any rate, dangerous and pro-
vocative rivalries, always dog the steps of humanity
until Christendom is one?

Personally, I think reunion with Rome is so far
off that it need not trouble us just now ; there are
other things to do ; but I would certainly refrain
from anything which made ultimate reunion more
difficult. And so I hold fast to my Catholic doctrines.
But I tell you where I find a great difficulty. A man
comes to me for adult baptism. I have to ask him,
point by point, if he verily believes the various
doctrines of the Church, doctrines which a man
baptised as an infant may not definitely accept
and yet remain a faithful member of Christ's Church.
What am I to say to one who has the passion of
Christian morality in his heart, but asks me whether
these verbal statements of belief are essential? He
might say to me, "It would be immoral to assert
that I believe what I have not examined, and to
examine this doctrine so thoroughly as to give an
answer not immoral would take a lifetime. Am I to
remain outside the Church till then ? " Here, I think,
the Church can take a step which would widen its
influence enormously. No man ought to be shut out
of Christ's Church who has the love of God and the

love of humanity in his heart. That seems to me quite clear. I don't like to say we make too much of the creeds, but I do say that we don't make half enough of the morality of Christ. That's where I should like to see the real test applied.

What I should like to see would be a particular and individual profession of the Beatitudes. I should like to see congregations stand up, face to the East, do anything, I mean, that marks this profession out as something essential and personal, and so recite the Beatitudes. There might be a great sifting, but it would bring home the reality of the Christian demand to the heart and conscience of the world. After all, that's our ideal, isn't it?—the City of God. If we all concentrated on this ideal, realising that the morality of Christ is essential, I don't think there would be much bother taken, outside professional circles, about points of doctrine.

Then, writes the interviewer, arose the question of fervour. " Can the City of God be established without some powerful impulse of the human heart ? Can it ever be established, for example, by the detached and self satisfied intellectual priggishness of the subsidised sixpenny review, or by the mere violence of the Labour extremist's oratory ? Must there not be something akin to the evangelical enthusiasm of the last century, something of a revivalist nature ? And yet have we not outgrown anything of the kind ?

" To Canon Temple the answer presents itself in this way : Rarer than Christian charity is Christian faith. The supreme realism is yet to come, namely, the realisation of Christ as a living Person, the realisation that He truly meant what He said, the realisation that what He said is of paramount importance in all the affairs of human life. When mankind becomes consciously aware of the Christian faith as a supreme truth, then there will be a realistic effort to establish the City of God. The first step, then, is for the Church to make itself something transcendently different from the materialistic world. It must truly mean what it says when it asserts the morality of Christ Blessed are the poor in spirit, the meek, the merciful, the pure in heart, the peacemakers. The fervour is not to be born of an individual fear of hell or an individual anxiety for celestial safety, but of an utterly unselfish enthusiasm for the welfare of the world."

I should give a false impression of this very interesting man, who is so sincere and so steadfast, if I did not mention the significant fact of his happiness. He has always struck me, in spite of his formidable intellect and a somewhat pedagogic front and the occasional accent of an ancient and scholarly ecclesiasticism, as one of the happiest and most boy-like of men—a man whose centre must be cloudlessly serene, and who finds life definitely good. His laughter indeed, is a noble witness to the truth of a rational and moral existence. His strength is as the strength of ten, not only because his heart is pure, but because he has formulated an intelligent thesis of existence.

He has pointed out that the Pickwick Papers could not have been produced in any but a Christian country. " Satire you may get to perfection in pagan countries. But only in those countries where the morality of Christ has penetrated deeply do you get the spirit that loves the thing it laughs at."

Chapter XI

PRINCIPAL W B. SELBIE

I make not therefore my head a grave, but a treasure of knowledge ; I intend no Monopoly, but a community in learning ; I study not for my own sake only, but for theirs that study not for themselves.

I envy no man that knows more than my self, but pity them that know less. I instruct no man as an exercise of my knowledge, or with an intent rather to nourish and keep it alive in mine own head, then beget and propagate it in his ; and in the midst of all my endeavour, there is but one thought that dejects me, that my acquired parts must perish with my self, nor can be Legacied among my honoured Friends.—Sir Thomas Browne.

Mansfield College, Oxford, has been happy in its Principals. Dr. Fairbairn created respect for Nonconformity in the very citadel of High Anglicanism ; Dr. Selbie has converted that respect into friendship. There is no man of note or power at Oxford who does not speak with real affection of this devoted scholar, who has been dubbed up there " an inspired mouse."

He is a little man, with quick darting movements, a twinkling bright eye, an altogether unaggressive voice, and a manner that is singularly insinuating and appealing. As it is impossible to think of a blustering or brow-beating mouse, or a mouse that advances with the stride of a Guardsman and the minatory aspect of a bull-terrier, so it is impossible to think of Dr. Selbie as a fellow of any truculence, a scholar of any prejudice, a Christian of any unctimoniousness. Mildness is the very temper of his soul, and modesty the centre of his being.

He is a Hebrew scholar who has advanced into philosophical territory and now is pushing his investigations into the field of psychology. Modest and wholly unpretentious he sets up as no original genius, and is content with his double rôle of close observer and respectful critic. He is rather a guide to men than a light. He has nothing new to say, but nothing foolish. His words are words of purest wisdom, though you may have heard them before. You feel that if he cannot lead you to the Promised Land, at least he will not conduct you to the precipice and the abyss.

Above everything else he is a scholar who would put his learning at the service of his fellow-men. Education with him is a passion, a part of his philanthropy, a part of his religion. It is the darkness of man, not the sinfulness of man, that catches his attention. He feels that the world is foolish because it is ignorant, not because it is wicked. And he feels that the foolishness of the world is a count in the indictment against religion. Religion has not taught; it has used mankind as a dictaphone.

He has spoken to me with great hope and confidence of the change which is coming over the Church in this matter of religious teaching. Dr.

Headlam, the Regius Professor of Divinity, has
lighted a candle at Oxford which by God's grace will
never be put out. There is now a fairly general
feeling that men who enter the ministry must be
educated not to pass a test or to prove themselves
capable of conducting a service or performing a
rite, but educated as educators—apostles of truth,
evangelists of the higher life.

Religion, according to Dr. Selbie, is something
to be taught. It is not a mystery to be presented,
but an idea to be inculcated. The world has got
to understand religion before it can live religiously.

But all education stands in sore need of the trained
teacher. Our teachers are not good enough. They
may be very able men and women, but few of them
are very able teachers. The first need in a teacher
is to inspire in his students a love of knowledge, a
hunger and thirst after wisdom. But, look at our
schools, look at our great cities, look at the pleasures
and recreations which satisfy the vast masses of
the population ! As a nation, we have no enthusiasm for education. This is because we have so
little understanding of the nature and province of
education. We have never been taught what
education is.

With his enthusiasm for education goes a per-
fervid spiritual conviction that intellect is not
enough. He tells the story of an old Scots woman
who listened intently to a highly intellectual sermon
by a brilliant scholar, and at the end of it called out
from her seat, " Aye, aye ; but yon rope o' yours
is nae lang enough tae reach the likes o' me."
Something much more mysterious and much more

powerful than intellect is necessary to change the heart of humanity ; but when love and knowledge go hand in hand there you get both the great teacher and the good shepherd. Knowledge without love is almost as useless to a teacher as love without knowledge.

In his study at Mansfield, a large and friendly room book-lined from floor to ceiling, with a pleasant hearth at one end of it, where he smokes an occasional pipe with an interrupting fellow scholar, but where he is most often to be found buried in a great book and oblivious of all else besides, this little man with the darting eyes and soft voice is now invading, with sound good sense to save him from nausea or contamination, the region of morbid psychology.

He would perfectly agree with Dr. Inge's characteristic statement, " The suggestion that in prayer we only hear the echo of our own voices is ridiculous to anyone who has prayed " ; but he is, I think, much more aware of the power and extent of this suggestion than is the Dean of St. Paul's, and therefore qualifies himself to meet the psychologists on their own ground.

He has confessed to me that in reading Freud he had to wade through much almost unimaginable filth, and he is driven to think that Freud himself is the victim of " a sex complex," a man so obsessed by a single theory, so ridden by one idea, that he perfectly illustrates the witty definition of an expert —" an expert is one who knows nothing else." All the same, Dr. Selbie assures me that his studies have been well worth while, that modern psychology has much to teach us of the highest value, and that religion as well as medicine will more and more have to take account of this daring science which advances so swiftly into their own provinces.

So far as my experience goes no man of the first rank in Anglican circles is preparing himself for this inevitable encounter with anything like the thoroughness of Dr. Selbie, a nonconformist.

He makes it a rule never to interfere with the troubles of another communion ; but I do not think I misrepresent him when I say that he regrets the immersion of the Church of England in questions of theological disputation at a time when the true battle of religion is shifting on to quite other ground.

Not many people in Anglo-Catholic circles realise perhaps that to the educated nonconformist all this excitement about modernism seems strangely old-fashioned. Long ago such matters were settled. The scholar nonconformist is no longer concerned with dogmatic difficulties; he has abandoned with the old teleology the old pagan theology, and now, believing in an immanent teleology, in an evolution that is creative and that has direction, believing also that Christ is the incarnation of God's purpose and the revelation of His character, he is pressing forward not to meet the difficulties of to-morrow, but to equip himself for meeting those difficulties when they arise with real intelligence and genuine power.

" If medicine," said Froude, " had been regulated three hundred years ago by Act of Parliament ; if there had been Thirty-Nine Articles of Physic, and every licensed practitioner had been compelled, under pains and penalties, to compound his drugs by the prescriptions of Henry the Eighth's physician, Doctor Butts, it is easy to conjecture in what state of health the people of this country would at present be found."

Christendom does not yet realise how greatly, how grievously, it has suffered in spiritual health by having sent to Coventry or to the stake so many theological Simpsons, Listers, and Pasteurs simply because they could not rest their minds in the hypotheses of very ill-educated men who strove to grapple with the highest of all intellectual problems at a time when knowledge was at its lowest level.

It will perhaps rouse the vitality of the Church when it finds twenty or thirty years from now that the great protagonists of Christianity in its future battles with science and philosophy are drawn from the ranks of nonconformity.

Dr. Selbie is certainly preparing his students for these encounters, and preparing them, too, with an emphasis on one particular aspect of the old theology, and a central one, which the apologists of more orthodox communions have either overlooked or find it convenient to ignore.

One of his first postulates is that man inhabits a moral universe, and from this postulate he has no difficulty in moving forward not only to contemplate the hypothesis of immortality, but to confront the difficulty of punishment for sin. In a little book of his called *Belief and Life* he has the following passages :

In the long last men cannot be persuaded to deny their own moral nature, and they will not be content

with a theory of the universe which does not satisfy
their sense of right.

And because of this very sense of right they
entertain no soft and sentimental notions concerning the universe :

> They believe in judgment, in retribution, and in the
> great principle that " as a man sows, so shall he also
> reap." They therefore require that room shall be
> found in the scheme of things for the working out of
> this principle. They recognise that such room is not
> to be found in this present life, and so they accept
> the fact that God hath set eternity in our hearts,
> and that we are built on a scale which requires a more
> abundant life to complete it.
> In corroboration of their faith, it may be said, as
> John Stuart Mill used to argue, that wherever belief
> in the future has been strong and vivid, it has made
> for human progress. There is no doubt that the
> deterioration of religion and the more material views
> of life so prevalent just now are due to the loss of
> faith in the future.

Religion, he says, can never live or be effective
within the narrow circle of time and sense. Nevertheless he has the courage to say : " The future
life, like the belief in God, is best treated as an
hypothesis that is yet in process of verification."
But this hypothesis explains what else were
inexplicable. It works. And, confronting the
hypothesis of immortality, he insists that a future
life must embrace retribution " As a man sows,
so shall he also reap." Immortality is not to be
regarded as a sentimental compensation for our
terrestrial experience, but as the essential continuity
of our spiritual evolution ' For many, no doubt,

it will mean an experience of probation, and for all one of retribution."

He sees clearly and gratefully that " the moral range of the work of Christ in the human soul, His gifts of grace, forgiveness, and power, lift men at once on to the plane of the spiritual and fill their conception of life with a new and richer content." But he does not shut his eyes to the fact of the moral law, and with all the force of his character and all the strength of his intellect he accepts " the great principle that as a man sows, so shall he also reap."

In this way Dr. Selbie prepares his students, not only to meet the intellectual difficulties of the future, but to stand fast in the ancient faith of their forefathers that the moral law is a fact of the universe. He helps them to be fighters as well as teachers. They are to fight the complacency of men, the false optimism of the world, the delusive tolerance of materialism. There is no need for them to preach hell fire and damnation, but through-out all their preaching, making it a real thing and a thing of the most pressing moment, must ring that just and inevitable word, Retribution. In a moral universe, selfishness involves, rightly and inevitably, suffering—suffering self-sown, self-deter-mined, and self-merited.

He is the last man in the world from whom one would expect such teaching to emanate. He seems, in his social moments, a scholar who is scarcely aware of humanity in his delicious pursuit of pure truth, a man who inhabits the faery realm of ideas, and drinks the milk of Paradise. But approach him on other ground and you find, though his serenity never deserts him, though he is always imperturbable and unassertive, that his interest in humanity and the practical problems of humanity is as vivid and consuming as that of any social reformer.

There, in Oxford, among his books, and carrying on his duties as Principal of Mansfield College, Dr. Selbie, back from holidays spent in watching the great working world and listening to the teachers of that world, finds himself not alarmed, but anxious. The voice of religion, he feels, is not making itself heard, and the voices of churches are making only a discord. Men are going astray because they have no knowledge of their course, and the blind are falling into the ditch because they are led by the blind. How is this dangerous condition of things to be remedied ?

He replies, By the teachers.

What we need at this hour above all other needs is the great teacher, one able to proclaim and explain the truths of religion, and filled with a high enthusiasm for his office. We need, he tells me, men who can restore to preaching its best authority. At the present time preaching has fallen to a low ebb because it is despised, and it is despised because it has lost the element of teaching. But let men recover their faith in the moral law, let them see that retribution is inevitable justice, let them realise that the life of man is a progress in spiritual comprehension, let them understand that existence is a great thing and not a mean thing, and they will feel again the compulsion to preach, and their preaching, founded on the moral law and inspired by faith in the teaching of Christ, will draw the world from the destructive negations of materialism, and wake it out of the fatal torpors of dull indifference.

Happy, I think, is the church which has such a teacher at the head of its disciples. Though its traditions may not reach far back into the historic twilight of ignorance, the rays of the unrisen sun strike upon its banners as they advance towards the future of mankind.

CHAPTER XII

ARCHBISHOP RANDALL DAVIDSON

Let us be flexible, dear Grace; let us be flexible!—
HENRY JAMES.
. . . the Archbishop recalled both to the gravity of the issue.—LORD MORLEY.

BECAUSE of his great place and his many merits, both of heart and head, and also because his career raises the question I desire to discuss in my Conclusion, I have left the Archbishop of Canterbury to the last of these brief studies in religious personality.

More admirably, I think, because more entirely, than any of the other men I have attempted to study, Dr. Davidson sums up the virtues of Anglicanism. He stands, first and foremost, for order, decency, and good temper. If he has a passion it is for the *status quo*. If he has a genius it is for compromise. Lord Morley, who knows him and respects him, describes him as " a man of broad mind, sagacious temper, steady and careful judgment, good knowledge of the workable strength of rival sections." Pre-eminently the Archbishop is a practical man.

I know not out of how many crises he has contrived, both as a fisher of men and a good shepherd, to lift the Church of England by hook or by crook.

When he was a youth a serious accident threatened to destroy his health and ruin his prospects. A charge of gunshot struck him at the bottom of the spine. The shot still remain in his body, and every autumn he is visited with an attack of quasi-peritonitis which reduces him to a sad state of weakness. For long weeks together—once it was for a whole year—his diet is restricted entirely to milk foods.

In spite of this grave disability, I am inclined to doubt if there is a harder worker in any church of the world. Dr. Davidson's knowledge of the Church of England, not only in these British Islands but in every one of the Dominions, is a knowledge of the most close and intimate nature. He knows the names and often the character of men who are working in the remotest parishes of the uttermost parts of the Empire. He knows also their thousand difficulties and is often at pains to relieve their distresses. This devotion has an ideal origin. He has cherished the dream all his life that the Church of England, so sane, so moderate, so sensible, and so rightly insistent on moral earnestness, may become, with the growth and development of the British Commonwealth, the greatest of all the Christian Churches—greater, more catholic, than Rome.

To this end he has worked with a devotion and a strain of energy which only those immediately about him can properly appraise.

Such is the exhaustion of this labour that when he can find time to take a day off he spends it in bed.

His policy has always been to keep men reasonable, but with no ignoble idea of living a quiet life.
His powers of persuasion, which have succeeded so
often in making unreasonable men temporarily
reasonable, have their source in the transparent
sincerity of his soul. No one who encounters him
can doubt for a moment that the Primate is seeking
the good of the Church of England, and seeking
that good because he believes in the English Church
as one of the great spiritual forces of civilisation.
No one, I mean, could think that he is either tem-
porising for the sake of peace itself or that his
policy of moderation masks a secret sympathy with
a particular party.   Clear as the sun at noon is
the goodness of the man, his unprejudiced devotion
to a practical ideal, and his unselfish ambition for
the reasonable future of the great Church of the
English nation.

He gives most of us the feeling of a very able
man of business, an ideal family solicitor ; but
there is a quite different side to his character.   He
is by no means a mystic, as that word is usually
understood, but he is a man who deeply believes in
the chief instrument of the mystic's spiritual life,
that is to say, in prayer.   He is not a saint, in the
general acceptance of that term, but his whole life
is devoted with an undeviating singleness of aim
to effecting the chief ambition of the saint—a knowledge of God in the hearts and minds of men.
Because he believes that the best method of achieving
that consummation, having regard to the present
level of human intelligence, is by moderate courses,
one must not think that he is lukewarm in the

cause of religion. With all the force of his clear and able mind, he believes in moderation. Anything that in the least degree savours of extravagance seems to him impolitic. He does not believe in sudden bursts of emotional energy ; he believes in constant pressure.

In my intercourse with him I have found him eminently sane and judicial, cold towards excessive fervour, but not cold at all towards ardent faith, inclined perhaps to miss the cause of spiritual impatience, constitutionally averse from any understanding sympathy with religious ecstasy, but never self-satisfied, intolerant, or in the remotest fashion cynical. Always he expresses his views with modesty, and sometimes with healthy good-humour, disposed to take life cheerfully, never moved to mistake a molehill for a mountain, always quietly certain that he is on the right road, whatever critics may care to say about his pace.

It is perhaps unreasonable to expect height and depth where there is excessive breadth. The Archbishop might make a bad captain, but he could have few rivals as an umpire. He is an admirable judge if an indifferent advocate.

His grave earnestness is balanced by a conviction that humour is not without a serious purpose. He looks upon life in the average, avoiding all abnormality, and he sees the average with a genial smile. He thoroughly appreciates the oddities of English character, and would ask with Gladstone, " In what country except ours (as I know to have happened) would a Parish Ball have been got up in order to supply funds for a Parish Hearse ? "

His attitude to the excitements and sensations of the passing day may be gathered from a simple incident. During the most heady days of the War, that is to say, days when people made least use of their heads, I encountered him at the country-house of a well-known statesman. One morning, while we were being lined up for a photograph, the boarhound of our host came and forced himself between the Archbishop and myself. " What would the newspapers say," exclaimed the Archbishop in my ear, " if they knew that his name is—*Kaiser* ! "

In this manner he regards all sensational excitement of every kind. When people are tearing their hair, and the welkin rings with such affrighting cries as Downfall and Crisis, the Archbishop's rather solemn and alarmed countenance breaks up into a genial smile. It is when people are immovable in otiose self-satisfaction, when the air is still and when lethargy creeps over the whole body of humanity, that the face of Dr. Davidson hardens. There is nothing he dreads more than apathy, nothing that so stimulates his policy of constant pressure as inertia. Ndengei, the supreme deity of the Fiji Islands, the laziest of all the gods, has the serpent for his effigy. " The Devil tempts the busy man," says a Turkish proverb, " but the idle man tempts the Devil."

One of those who has worked with the Archbishop for many years, although his views are of a rather extreme order and his temperament altogether of the excessive kind, said to me the other day, " When Randall Davidson went to Canterbury, I told those who asked me what would be the result of his reign,

He will leave the Church as he found it. I was wrong. He has done much more than that." He went on to say that there was now a far greater charity between the different schools than existed at the beginning of the century, and that if unity had not been attained, at least disruption had been avoided.

One of the most eloquent and far-sighted of the Evangelicals puts the matter to me in this fashion : " It is possible that fifty years hence men may ask whether he ought not to have been constructive ; but for the present we, his contemporaries, must confess that it is wonderful how he keeps things together."

" Pull yourself together ! " was the admonition addressed to a somewhat hilarious undergraduate. " But I haven't got a together," he made answer.

If it be true that a house divided against itself cannot stand, then we must admit that Dr. Randall Davidson is not merely one of the Church's greatest statesmen, but a worker of miracles, a man whom we might expect to take up serpents and drink any deadly thing.

But it will be safe to keep the Archbishop's reputation in the region of statesmanship.

The reader, I hope, will not think me either pedantic or supercilious if I insist that no word is more misused by the newspapers, indeed by the whole modern world, than this word statesmanship. It is a word of which the antonym is drifting. It signifies steersmanship, and implies control, guidance, direction, and, obviously, foresight. Now, let us see how this word is used by those who are supposed to instruct public opinion.

The settlement of the Irish Question was hailed as a triumph of British statesmanship. One of the Sunday newspapers of the higher order acclaimed Mr. Lloyd George as the greatest statesman in the history of England and perhaps the greatest man in the world. But it needs only a little thought, only a moment's reflection, to realise that this welcome settlement was a triumph, not of statesmanship, but of murderous brutality. There would have been no pæans if there had been no volleys, no triumph if there had been no violence.

Statesmanship was defeated in the eighties, and those who defeated it, those who exalted prejudice and racialism and intolerance above rationality and foresight, are now among those whom the world salutes as immortal statesmen. In truth, they have bowed the knee to violence.

By the same power, and not by reason, the Government extended the franchise to women. Statesmanship held firmly on the contrary course till the winds of violence rose and the rain of anarchy threatened to descend in a flood of moral devastation.

Look closely into the great achievements of the Washington Conference and you will find that the nations are not voluntarily seeking the rational ideal of peace, but are being driven by urgent necessity into the course of reason. Statesmanship would have disarmed the world before 1914. It was only after 1918 that the spectre of Universal Bankruptcy drove the poor trembling immortals who pass for statesmen to embrace each other as heroes in search of an ideal. Humanity has achieved nothing noble or glorious in the last thirty years ;

it has been driven by the winds of God into every haven which has saved it from shipwreck.

With a clear understanding of the meaning of the word statesmanship, one may ask with some hope of arriving at an intelligent answer whether Randall Davidson is a great statesman.

Under his rule a divided and distracted Church has held together; but religion has gone out of favour. During his reign at Lambeth there has been a sensible movement towards reunion; but the nation is uninterested. If the Romanists have been less rebellious, the Evangelicals have lost almost all their zeal. If the Church still witnesses to the truth of Christianity, it is with all her ancient inequalities thick upon her, turning her idealism to ridicule, and in the midst of a nation which has become steadily more and more indifferent to the Church, more and more cynical towards religion.

If there is peace in the Church, there is little of that moral earnestness in the life of the nation which in past times laid the foundations both of English character and of English greatness. We are becoming swiftly, I think, a light and flippant people, the only seriousness in our midst the economic seriousness of our depressed classes. It is not to any other class in the community that the zealot can address himself with an evangel of any kind. Only where a sense of bitterness exists, a sense of anger and rebellion, can the idealist in these dangerous times hope for attention.

The Bishop of Manchester preached some few weeks ago a sermon to the unemployed of that city.

He was asked at the end of his sermon if the workers could get justice without the use of force. He replied, " It all depends what you mean by force." And at that the congregation shouted, " Murder." They were to have concluded the service with the hymn, " When wilt Thou save Thy people ? " Instead, it concluded with the singing of " The Red Flag."

Now let us ask ourselves what might have been the course of religious history during the last twenty years if Dr. Randall Davidson, instead of contenting himself with composing clerical quarrels, had used his high office to control the Church and to steer it in the direction of greater spiritual realism.

Suppose, for example, that after presiding over a conference of warring Churchmen, he had turned to one of the champions of a party, and had said to him, in the manner of a true spiritual father, " I have something to ask of you. What was the first command of our Risen Lord to the apostle Simon Peter ? " He would have been obliged to answer, " Feed My lambs." " And the second command ? " And he would have been obliged to say, " Feed My sheep." " And the third command ? " And again he would have been obliged to say, " Feed My sheep." Then, what had they all said if the Primate had turned to both sides and admonished them in these words, " My brothers in Christ, I think there would now be no disputation among you if instead of concerning yourselves with the traditions of men you had rather given yourselves entirely to obeying the commandment of our Risen Lord "?

But the question would remain, With what food is the flock to be fed?

Is it possible to give an answer to this question which will not open again the floodgates of controversy? If that is so, then those of us who acknowledge the moral law had better abandon Christianity altogether, and set ourselves to construct a new and unifying gospel of ethics from the works of the moralists. For the world is torn asunder by strife, and contention is the opportunity of the wolves. Humanity has begun to apprehend this truth. It has begun to find out that disarmament is practical wisdom; and now it is beginning to wonder whether counsels of perfection may not serve its domestic interests with a higher efficiency than the compromises effected by unprincipled politicians. It is in the mood to listen to a teacher who speaks with authority; but in no mood to listen to a war of words.

If religion cannot speak with one voice in the world, it had better adjourn, like the plenipotentiaries of Sinn Fein and the representatives of the British Government, to a secret session. It must come to an understanding with itself, an agreement as to what it means, before mankind will recover interest in its existence.

Chapter XIII

CONCLUSION

The fashion of this world passes away, and it is with what is abiding that I would fain concern myself.—GOETHE.

The breadth of my life is not measured by the multitude of my pursuits, nor the space I take up amongst other men ; but by the fulness of the whole life which I know as mine.—F. H. BRADLEY.

We are but at the very beginning of the knowledge and control of our minds ; but with that beginning an immense hope is dawning on the world.—" THE TIMES."

The Ideal is only Truth at a distance.—LAMARTINE.

IT is curious, if Christianity is from heaven, that it exercises so little power in the affairs of the human race.

Far from exercising power of any noticeable degree, it now ceases to be even attractive. The successors of St. Paul are not shaping world policy at Washington ; they are organising whist-drives and opening bazaars. The average clergyman, I am afraid, is regarded in these days as something of a bore, a wet-blanket even at tea-parties.

Something is wrong with the Church. It is impious to think that heaven interposed in the affairs of humanity to produce that ridiculous mouse, the modern curate. No teacher in the history of the world ever occupied a lower place in the respect of men. So deep is the pit into which the modern minister has fallen that no one attempts to get him out. He is abandoned by the world. He figures with the starving children of Russia in appeals to the charitable—an object of pity. The hungry sheep look up and are not fed, but the shepherd also looks up from his pit of poverty and neglect, as hungry as the sheep, hungry for the bare necessities of animal life.

This is surely a tragic position for a preacher of good news, and a teacher sent from God.

If the Christian would know how far his Church has fallen from power, let him reflect that, even after the sorrow and desolation of a world conflict, there is no atmosphere in Europe rendering the savagery of submarine warfare unthinkable—utterly unthinkable to the conscience of mankind.

Mr. Balfour and Lord Lee make a proposal to end this devilish warfare ; the French oppose ; newspapers open a crusade, here against France, there against Great Britain ; the vital interests of humanity are at stake ; the door will either be opened to disarmament or closed against peace for another fifty years ; and Christ is silent—the Church does not lift even three fingers to bless the cause of peace.

Why is the Church so powerless ? Why is it she has so fatally lost the attention of mankind ?

Is it not because she has nothing to give, nothing

to teach ? Morals are older than Christianity, and
sacramental religions as well. Men feel that they
cannot understand the immense paraphernalia of
religion and its unnatural atmosphere of high
mystery ; it is so tremendous a fuss about so very
small a result. If God is in the Church, why doesn't
He do more for it, and so more for the world ? The
revenues of religion are still enormous. What do
they accomplish ?

Men who think in this way are not enemies of
religion, any more than the Jews who came to Jesus
were enemies of Judaism. They deserve the respect
of the Church. Indeed, it is in finding an answer
to their challenge that the Church is most likely to
find a solution to her own problem. But that
answer will never be found if the Church seeks for
it only in her documents. There is another place
in which she must look for the truth of Christ, a
truth as completely overlooked by the modernist
as by the traditionalist : it is in the movements of
the soul, in the world of living men.

I believe that there are more evidences for the
existence of Christ in the modern world than in
the whole lexicon of theology. I believe it is more
possible to discern His features and to feel the
breath of His lips by confronting the discoveries
of modern science than by turning back the leaves
of religious history to the first blurred pages of the
Christian tradition. I believe, indeed, that it is
now wholly impossible for any man to comprehend
the Light which shone upon human darkness
nearly two thousand years ago without bringing
the documents of the Church to the light which

is shining across the world at this present hour from the torch of science.

" Why seek ye the living among the dead ? "

For twenty years I have followed this clue to the meaning of Christ and the nature of His message. I have seen Darwinism, the very foundation of modern materialism, break up like thin ice and melt away from the view of philosophy. I have seen evolution betray one of its greatest secrets to the soul of man—an immanent teleology, an invisible *direction* towards deeper consciousness, an intelligent *movement* towards greater under-standing. And I have seen the demonstration by science that this visible and tangible world in its final analysis is both invisible and intangible—a phantasm of the senses.

I may be allowed perhaps to recall the incident which first set me to follow this clue.

One day, when he was deep in his studies of Radiant Matter, Sir William Crookes touched a little table which stood between our two chairs, and said to me, " We shall announce to the world in a year or two, perhaps sooner, that the atoms of which this table is composed are made up of tiny charges of electricity, and we shall prove that each one of those tiny electrons, relative to its size, is farther away from its nearest neighbour than our earth from the nearest star."

I have lived to see this prophecy fulfilled, though its implications are not yet understood.

The Church does not yet realise that physical science, hitherto regarded as the enemy of religion and the mocker of philosophy, presents us now

with the world of the transcendentalists, the world
of the metaphysicians, the world of religious seers—
a world which is real and visible only to our limited
senses, but a world which disappears from all vision
and definition directly we bring to its investigation
those ingenious instruments of science which act
as extensions of our senses.

Every schoolboy is now aware that a door is solid
only to his eyes and touch ; that with the aid of
X-rays it becomes transparent, the light passing
through it as water passes through network, reveal-
ing what is on the other side. Every schoolboy
also knows that his own body can be so photo-
graphed as to reveal its skeleton.

But the Church has yet to learn from M. Bergson
the alphabet of this new knowledge, namely, that
our senses and our reason are what they are because
of a long evolution in *action*—not in pure thought.
We have got our sight by looking for prey or for
enemies, and our hearing by listening for the movement of prey or of enemies. Our reason, too, is
fashioned out of a long heredity of action, that is
to say an immemorial discipline in an existence
purely animal. So powerful is the influence of
this heredity, so real seems to us a physical world
which is not real, so infallible seem to us the senses
by which we fail to live successfully even as animals,
that, as Christ said, a man must be born again
before he can enter the Kingdom of God—that is
to say, before he can behold and inhabit Reality.

At the head of this chapter I have set a quota-
tion from a leading article in *The Times* on the
recent lectures of M. Coué. It is now eighteen

years ago, treading in the footsteps of Frederic Myers, that I discussed with some of the chief medical hypnotists in London and Paris the phenomena of mental suggestion. It was known then that auto-suggestion is a force of tremendous power. It was stated then that " an immense hope is dawning on the world," but not then, not even now, is it realised that this awkward term of " auto-suggestion " is merely a synonym for the more beautiful and ancient words, meditation and prayer.

We know now that a man can radically change his character, can uproot the toughest habits of a lifetime, by telling himself that his will is master in his house of life.[1] And we think that we have made this discovery, forgetting that Shakespeare said " The love of heaven makes us heavenly," and that Christ said, " Blessed are they which do hunger and thirst after righteousness : for they shall be filled," and " All things, whatsoever ye shall ask in prayer, believing, ye shall receive," or, as Mark has it, " What things soever ye desire, when ye pray, believe that ye receive them, and ye shall have them," and " According to your faith be it unto you."

With our present knowledge of the universe and of the human mind, it is at last possible for us to perceive in the confused records of the New Testament the nature of Christ's teaching. He loved the world for its beauty, but He penetrated its delusions and breathed the air of its only reality. " Lay not up for yourselves treasures upon the

---

[1] At Nancy even a lesión has been cured by suggestion.

earth . . . but lay up for yourselves treasures
in heaven . . . for where your treasure is, there
will your heart be also." " What is a man profited, if
he shall gain the whole world, and lose his own
soul ? or what shall a man give in exchange for his
soul ? " " If thou canst believe, all things are
possible to him that believeth." " He that hath
ears to hear let him hear."

His world was always the world of thought. The
actual deed of sin was merely a physical consequence ; the cause was spiritual : it was an evil
thought ; to harbour an evil thought is to commit
the sin. He looked into the hearts of men, into
their thoughts, and there only He found their
reality. All else was transitory. All else would
see corruption and die. The flesh profiteth nothing.
But the thought of a man—that is to say the region
now being explored by the psycho-analyst, the
psycho-therapeutist, and the psycho I know not
what else—this was the one region in which Jesus
moved, the region in which He proclaimed his
transvaluation of values, a region of which He
was so complete a master that He could heal delusion
at a word and disorder by a touch.

One does not perhaps wholly realise, until one
has read the muddied works of modern psychology,
how sublime was the soul of Jesus. It might be
possible to infer His divinity from the simplicity
of the language and the white purity of the thought
with which He expressed truths of the profoundest
significance even in regions where so many fall into
unhealthiness. " No man can serve two masters "
--is not that the teaching of the modern hypnotist

in dealing with " a divided self " ? " Set your affections on things above "—is not that the counsel of the sane psycho-analyst in treating a diseased mind ? " Ask, and it shall be given you ; seek, and ye shall find ; knock, and it shall be opened unto you "—is not this the message of M. Coué, the teaching of auto-suggestion ?—that teaching which makes us say at last that " an immense hope is dawning on the world."

And, in sober truth, we may indeed believe that this immense hope is dawning on the world ; the hope that mankind may recognise in Jesus, Who called Himself the Light of the World, the world's great Teacher of Reality.

Here we approach that unifying principle which was the object of our quest in setting out to explore the chaos of opinion in the modern Church.

Is it not possible that the Church might see the trivial unimportance of all those matters which at present dismember her, if she saw the supreme importance of Christ as a Teacher ? Might she not come to behold a glory in that Teaching greater even than that which she has so heroically but so unavailingly endeavoured to make the world behold in the crucified Sacrifice and Propitiation for its sins ?

Is there not here the opportunity of an evangel, the dawning of an immense hope on the world ?

But let the Church ask herself, before she abandons her labour of expounding doctrines concerning the Person of Christ, whether she is quite clear as to the teaching of Jesus. " Not every one that saith unto Me, Lord, Lord, shall enter into the Kingdom of Heaven ; but he that doeth the will of My Father which is in heaven."

Read St. Mark, the earliest, the least corrupted, of the narratives. It is a declaration of a new power in human life, and a record of its achievements. It is this, and nothing else. The one great word of that gospel is Faith—not faith in a formula or an institution, but faith in the absolute supremacy of spirit. Faith in spirit means power—power over circumstance, power over matter, power over the heredity of our animal origin. Jesus not only sets men free from the prison-house of material delusion, as Plato and others sought to do ; He teaches them the way in which alone they can exercise spiritual dominion.

There were two things to which He set no limits : one, the love of God, and the other, the power of Faith.

Let all the schools in the Church revise their definition of the word *faith*, and unity will come of itself. Faith, as Jesus employed that term, meant *making use of belief*—belief that the spiritual alone is the real. Faith is the action of the soul. It is the working of a power. It is mastery of life.

Let the Church realise that Jesus taught this power of the soul. Let her begin to exercise her own spiritual powers. And then let her understand that she is in the world to teach men, to lead the advance of evolution, to educate humanity in the use of its highest powers.

A knowledge of the sense in which Jesus employed the word Faith is the clue to the recovery of Christian influence.

This is the suggestion which I venture to submit to the Church, at a moment in history when the harsh and brutal spirit of materialism is crushing all faith out of the soul and leaving the body no tenant but its appetites.

I do not think any observant man can deny that the whole " suggestion " of the modern world is of an evil nature, that is to say, of a nature which fastens upon the mind the delusions of the senses, making it believe that what it sees is reality, persuading it that the gratification of those senses is the end and object of existence.   The wages of this suggestion is death—the death of the soul.

How far the world is gone from sanity, and how clearly science endorses Christ's teaching, may be seen in the modern craze for unhealthy excitement, and in the medical condemnation of that morbid passion.   A well-known doctor in London, Sir Bruce Bruce-Porter, has lately condemned Grand Guignol as intensifying the emotion of fear or anxiety— " Take no heed "—and has declared anger, or any violence of feeling, to be a danger—" Love your enemies "—pointing out that " the experiment of inoculating a guinea-pig with the perspiration taken from the forehead of a man in a violent temper has resulted in the death of the guinea-pig with all the symptoms of strychnine poisoning."

Science is the one voice that condemns in these days the self-destroying madness of a world set on seeking to live habitually in the lower life.   Sometimes journalism may light a candle of reason in our darkness, as when *The Times* recently pointed out in a leading article that the half-humorous interest

of the world in the murderer Landru had its
rise in a profound instinct of the human spirit,
namely, that horror must be laughed at if it is not
to be feared—to fear it is to be overwhelmed by it
This instinct is " an unconscious refusal to believe
in the ultimate reality of evil ; it is the predecessor
of the scientific spirit which says that evil is something to be overcome by understanding it."

Out of such a lethargy as that which now holds
her captive, I do not think the Church can be roused
except by the trumpets of war. Let her, then,
consider whether there is not here, in this world of
false values, of low ambitions, of mean pleasures,
of dark materialism, and of perilous superstitions,
a world to be fought, as the doctors fight it, and the
best kind of newspapers, if only for the sake of
posterity, a world against which it is good to oppose
oneself—the Children of Light against the Children
of Darkness.

What is the good news of Christianity if it is not
the news that " the spiritual alone is the real," that
there is freedom for human life and mastery for the
human soul, that faith in the spiritual is power over
the material ? Even in the tentative form which
M. Bergson uses to reveal the reality of the spiritual
world there is such joy that one of his interpreters
can exclaim :

> Here we are in these regions of twilight and dream,
> where our ego takes shape, where the spring within
> us gushes up, in the warm secrecy of the darkness
> which ushers our trembling being into birth. Distinc-
> tions fail us. Words are useless now. We hear the
> wells of consciousness at their mysterious task like
> an invisible shiver of running water through the

mossy shades of the caves. I dissolve in the joy of becoming. I abandon myself to the delight of being a pulsing reality. I no longer know whether I see scents, breathe sounds, or smell colours. Do I love? Do I think? The question has no longer a meaning for me. I am, in my complete self, each of my attitudes, each of my changes. It is not my sight which is indistinct or my attention which is idle. It is I who have resumed contact with pure reality, whose essential movement admits no form of number.

How much greater the joy of him who knows that Reality is God, and that God is Father.

> The open secret flashes on the brain,
> As if one almost guessed it, almost knew
> Whence we have sailed and voyage whereunto.

Let us suppose that the whole Church of Christ was engaged in teaching men this high mystery, this open secret, that all such great associations as the Christian Students' Movement, the Adult Sunday School Movement, the World Association for Adult Education, and all the numerous Missionary Societies throughout the whole earth—let us suppose that the entire Church of Christ was at work in the world teaching Christ's teaching, *educating* men, bringing it home to the heart and mind of humanity that " life is mental travel," that it is in our thoughts we live and by our thoughts we are shaped, that flesh and blood cannot inherit the Kingdom of God, that all terrestrial values are radically false, that to hunger and thirst after anything is to get it, that the power of " the dominant wish " is our fate, that in love alone can we live to the full stature of our destiny, that the Kingdom of God is within us, that the engine of faith has not yet been exerted by the whole human race in concert, that conquests await us in the spiritual world before which all the conquests of the material world will pale into insignificance, that we are spirits finding our way out of the darkness of an animal ancestry into the Light of an immortal inheritance as children of God ; let us suppose that this, and not dogma, was the Voice of the Church ; must we not say that by such teaching the whole world would eventually be rescued from our present chaos and in the fulness of time be born again into the knowledge of spiritual reality ?

I believe it is only when a man realises that in its final analysis the whole universe is invisible, and ceases to think of himself as an animal and becomes profoundly sensible of himself as a spirit, and a spirit in communion with a spiritual reality closer than hands and feet, that it is possible for him to fulfil the two great commandments on which hang all the Law and the Prophets. And without that fulfilment there must always be chaos.

If the Church will not teach the world, modern science will inspire philosophy to take up anew the teaching of Plato, and the world will go forward into the light, but with no creative love in its soul to save it from itself. " If therefore," said Christ, " the light that is in thee be darkness, how great is that darkness."